Feng Shui
Your Mind

LIFE COACH FOR ABUNDANCE

J.J. LUPI

BALBOA.
PRESS

A DIVISION OF HAY HOUSE

Balboa Press books may be ordered through booksellers or by contacting:
Balboa Press
A Division of Hay House
1663 Liberty Drive
Bloomington, IN 47403
www.balboapress.com
1-(877) 407-4847

Printed in the United States of America.

ISBN: 978-1-4525-7818-7 (sc)
ISBN: 978-1-4525-7828-6 (hc)
ISBN: 978-1-4525-7819-4 (e)

Library of Congress Control Number: 2013913124

Balboa Press rev. date: 12/20/2013

To my sons,

Zé

João

Teresa

Luz

For the things I learned with them ....

TABLE OF CONTENTS

FOREWORD

Understand the mysteries of life was a journey I started 36 years ago, after getting a solid scientific background in some of the best European universities and working as international researcher on ICT information and communication technology and its psycho sociological implementation in human contexts.

This scientific background was then complemented through deepening the understanding of human nature, based on studies of neurolinguistic programming and coaching with its founders and masters in the US and Europe. This allowed me to understand humans and their behavior, but I knew there was more to it.

Moving to China and Asian countries allowed me to contact with eastern philosophy and the holistic and more spiritual approaches to life dimensions, namely through the Feng Shui studies I followed throughout China, USA and European Schools. Through this journey I could integrate the main dimensions of life, Heaven and Earth, together with our Space tridimensional (3D) environment, and Time as the 4th dimension.

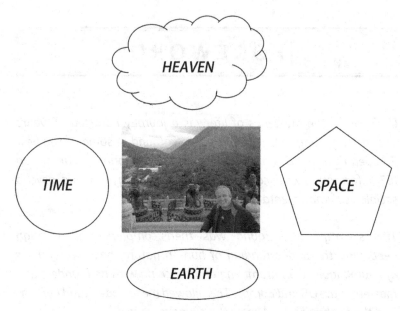

Man Between Heaven and Earth: the life dimensions

Through this process I could integrate the western techniques of personal development and change, in a wider context on questions like the balance between free will and predestination, synchronicity and time management, with life as it is, to create the NEURO FENG SHUI Coach, as a powerful Life Management Tool, that you can use by yourself to improve your life, making sense of it, define and achieve your goals, and live with abundance, in peace and harmony with yourself in all your dimensions.

Curiously, I finished this book in between east and west, in Tangarog.

Summer solstice, full moon of June 2013

J.J. Lupi

OVERVIEW

A practical guide to Life Coach for Abundance for common citizens, this book is a complete step by step Self Coach process that will show you how to integrate your surrounding energies and your innermost drives, in a very easy and friendly way.

We will give you the tools and secrets, on how to blend the eastern awareness of subtle energies and the western mind, to approach a subtle inner and outer world containing the very essence of your quality of life and personal well-being. This is your door to a world of Personal Power, Liberation and Co-Creation of a great life!

When East meets West, we find Feng Shui and our Mind Programs

Feng Shui, is deeply based on the two major philosophical schools of China: Confucius (Kong Zi, 551 – 479 AC), creator of Confucianism, and Lao Tse (Lao Zi), of the Taoism. Feng Shui integrates these ancient awareness with all modern concepts of ergonomics, architecture, physic and quantum mechanics.

This ancient oriental art of Space Acupuncture, handles the subtle relationships of man with his environment, and it arrived in the 70's to the Western world with Master Li Yun in California, with the School of **Feng Shui** known as the of the BTB (Black Hat Tibetan Buddhism), after passing from its birthplace in China, to India where it was enriched by Vastu, and through Tibet where it gained a more spiritual component.

Feng Shui is the branch of the I Ching system that studies cosmological and geological influences on our vitality and prosperity. To master the art of traditional Feng Shui, one must hold great knowledge and skills of mathematics', symbolism (Xiang 象) and numerology (Shu 數).

In Feng Shui we evaluate the environmental energies that surround us, like the shapes of a landscape, a home, an office, or another building with any specific intended usages; starting from the external environment, then we move on, and evaluate all the aspects of the site, from the general perspective to organize its internal space, in every room, in order to build up, the energies most need through the so called Feng Shui "cures".

We know empirically and even scientifically today the impact of the macro world, the galaxy's, the atmosphere, the earth, our neighbors, our location, our house, our office, our colleagues, our family, and all the rest of our environment in our lifes, our body and our cells.

The ancient esoteric teachings of Hermes Trimegistus, are now fully confirmed since the emergency one hundred years ago, of the new physics and quantum mechanics, stating that we live in a holographic universe where every single particle contains information of the whole, so the whole is identical to its parts, and all is equal, from top to bottom, macro and micro, from the organization of the universe to the organization of our cells, atoms and subatomic space. From the infinitely large to the infinitely small, it illustrates well the interrelation of all that exists.

As Above, so below

The Yellow Emperor

Space Acupuncture

**Acupuncture Points for
Chinese and Russian
Empires**

The author in Beijin's Temple of Heaven and Red Square in Moscow

Fig 1

Modern Chinese daily life is still impregnated with Feng Shui tradition, even if it is so embedded in their culture that the main rules are unconsciously adopted, in a natural way, despite its prohibition during the Cultural Revolution.

You can see this natural way, through the usage off hexagonal mirrors as a Ba Gua symbol for protection outside the windows to reflect bad Feng Shui, or the Buddhist altars with food and incense practices, or the avoidance of number four (4), which in Cantonese sounds like "dead" so it is considered an unfortunate number, or even the dislike of the color blue because it is used in the Chinese funeral lanterns.

The programs in your mind

The peripheral nervous system, has around 100 million receptors to capture your reality, namely through your five senses, seeing, earing, sensing, smell and taste, but your brain connections between neurons are more than 10.000.000 million, so your internal information is more than 100.000 times bigger than the external information.

This informational nervous system is responsible to connect these internal and external information with our body-mind reactions mostly through the muscles and the hormones. This is how your mind creates your reality from your external stimulus to your dreams and memories, real or invented.

The techniques of Neuro-Linguistic Programming (NLP), and coaching, analyze and organize our "Inner Space", and whether in space acupuncture, we deal with the outside world, here we deal with the ability to program and reprogram the way human mind and body work together, in quick noninvasive ways.

In the early 70's the main techniques to access the "Human Inner Space", were born at the same time than oriental culture arrived to western countries, and from then on, we assisted, especially during the last 20 years, to the discovery of more than 90% of what we know and guess today regarding the potential capabilities and functioning of our conscious and unconscious minds, within what is already considered as the "century of the mind".

Feng Shui your Mind

The unique approach of this book, will show you how to use the Feng Shui matrix to analyze the environment, to access the strategies, framework and energy channels, that reorganize your life. The concepts of Feng Shui, for the external energies of landscape and buildings, will be the starting point and then zooming in, into your house and office, your human network, body and mind, and finally your Life Settings.

A simple "Life Coach" Guide for Abundance, this book is full of exercises to evaluate and balance the situations in your life, your mind, body and soul, and provide you everything you need to set up your life and live happily ever after.

First, the concepts and tools, you will be introduced to the main principles of energy sensing and managing with the tools and concepts for managing your home and work environment. This will allow you to be aware of the invisible forces that are present and influence your life, and playing a decisive role when making you a winner or a looser.

Earthly matters will be dealt with in Feng Shui your Environment, to organize your space at home and work, creating a supportive surrounding for an abundant and happy life.

Next, the Human realm, where each one of your life domains will be checked with maps and exercises, highlighting its main patterns and every time, tools and techniques are provided to reinforce and balance each area, of your Life Feng Shui.

The third level is your Personal Feng Shui, because life has predestination and free will and movement, where impermanence is the rule, so we will provide you the knowledge of the secret types of personality and life cycles, as a support tool to evaluate your main unconscious strengths, weaknesses, opportunities and threats in each life period.

The secret path of the Flying Stars, will show you the calculation and analysis of your best directions, Gua number, pillars of destiny and their evolution along your life path, also belonging to your faith, predetermination or heaven's luck, that shape your destiny.

To disclose your unconscious drives, and stimulate your self-awareness and intuition, we will present an introduction to the usage of the "I Ching" or the Book of Changes and the calculation of your life hexagram revealing your main life path energy, based on the hidden knowledge on how to access your unconscious awareness.

Your Human network of friends and relatives are a main frame for your life wellbeing, so this part will offer you the maps to check compatibilities and manage your important relations with partners, friends and intimate relationships.

Finally we will give you access to a Life Coaching process, where you will learn how to integrate the above three dimensions in an operative master plan to understand the actual situation, drives and subjacent processes of your life, thus providing the specific solutions and markers of your Road to Success and Abundance in your life.

Each part will end with a protocol on how to use that information in a summary check list related to those tools. The full case study with all calculations is presented in the Annex at the end of the book.

Overview: the Science of Coaching and the Art of Feng Shui

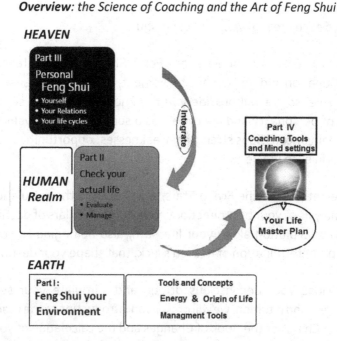

"The Art of Feng Shui begins where the Science of Coaching ends"

PART I

Feng Shui your environment and the origins of life

PART I

Feng Shui your Environment and the Origins of Life

We start providing you, the main concepts on the origin of life and how energy impacts every area of it, based on the awareness and eastern knowledge since the beginning of times from the oriental philosophers and Feng Shui practitioners.

This will allow you to be initiated to the world of subtle energies sensing and mapping, which concerns the influence of nature and the environment on human fortune, in its home, work, social, and spiritual life.

Heaven and earth, the Yin Yang, the four seasons, the five elements, the eight natural phenomena, and geographical directions, all are the natural basis of the environment energies that shape our life in a permanent interaction.

Your environment is mostly influenced by Time and Space, so the full understanding of its impact needs to integrate at least

- (1) the nature of the Universe,
- (2) the concepts of Space, and
- (3) the concepts of Time.

We will check all this dimensions with examples and tools to access and adjust your fortune to threats and opportunities.

The "Feng Shui of the Environment", deals with how we are affected by visible and tangible things that surround us, so we will work with the major techniques on how to sense, understand and act, over the main structures of our reality, like the geographical location of properties, your house with each of its rooms, the design, the furniture, the directions you face, colors, clothes, attitudes, office and its organization.

During the second part of the book, we check all life dimensions based on the Feng Shui Wheel of Life, reviewing each of them, from your root patterns and origins, to your children, home, work and social dimensions, with people and situations that surround us and we face every day, and are mirrors of our own energy.

Finally, we will have a deep look, through our Personal Feng Shui, showing where we come from, our helpful and compatible directions, together with the best people to surround us as our human support network, with tools like the I Ching "the Book of Changes", Pillars of Destiny, and the Flying Stars.

An easy Life Coach Protocol, in the last part, will summarize the way to integrate all the above information allowing you to help yourself to live at the edge, identifying where you are, stating clearly where you go, implementing changes, achieving and monitoring your goals.

1

Energy and the Origins of life

How can you live a happy and fortunate life, in the middle of the uncertainties of modern civilization?

You access here the *best of two worlds widely* recognized of **Eastern knowledge and Western technology**, these are the top world resilient tools to raise your awareness and balance during current times. Only Awareness, together with the best knowledge and tools available for mind control at your disposal can give you the best chances to succeed in the actual life scenarios.

Eastern philosophy and the holistic view of life and its mysteries, are the approach most resistant to time proof, as acupuncture, which in the last 5.000 years of existence, is the most tested of actual healing methods.

The energy approach of life, based on the vital force, called Chi in china, Prana in India, crossed the Himalayas, and arrived into western world embedded in spirituality, practices and culture, since the visit of The US president Nixon to Mao Tse Tung's China and was fostered by the exode to India, of Tibetan monks after the political changes in the government of that region.

Simultaneously, the western countries following the industrial revolution, took a world lead for the first time in history, with technology facing a surge since the beginning of XX century in

Europe and the USA, where quantum mechanics and technology, computers and knowledge of the human mind develop with several Nobel Prizes, and allowed as never seeing before, the emergency of brain and mind discoveries, concerning human behavior, brain, and neuro linguistic programming. This hard and soft technologies, started a huge movement to empowerment of self, through understanding manage our own reality and create our Lives and liberty, beyond usual boundaries.

We provide you in the next pages a practical and simple access to this methods and tools, where you get a totally new approach to life, it's secrets and triggers in order to understand, dissolve, and create, adjustments and balance in all areas in your life pack, keeping a clear alignment with your purpose, focus on your targets, and a useful attitude at all times as the basis or your most efficient decisions at every moment of your life experience.

Let's start this journey describing the genesis of energy Chi, explained by Feng Shui, from its traditional view embedded in Eastern philosophy.

Water and Wind... changing from the calm, of a late afternoon, when the heat emanating from the Earth is attenuated by a gentle breeze, to the glow of a storm, at high sea where tidal waves intersect with the howling of cyclonic winds, in the midst of darkness in which thunder flashes and lightning bolts duel. The extreme opposites of this nature elements, show clearly how different is their impact according to the mix and balance among them.

Perfect illustration of how the bipolar states of a restless and uneasy mind, are the opposite mirror effect of a stable attitude that comes from emotional balance, where every emotion is lived fully as a sign of harmony, and warnings of deviations in one's life path, or in the opposite end, contradictory thoughts collapse with beliefs and assumptions that go against the reality, and yet continue to respond impulsively against all evidence of meeting expectations, or the desired goals.

Becaming aware of your external and internal environment, you start sensing subtle energies around you. Each of these energies has two dimensions: its "quality" and its "quantity".

Energy in motion

In the beginning there was Unity, the "All That Exists" symbolized by the Circle.

"There is thing, formless yet complete that existed before Heaven and Earth ...

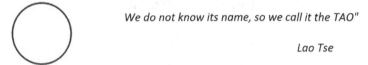

We do not know its name, so we call it the TAO"

Lao Tse

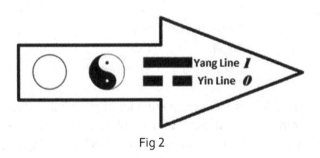

Fig 2

With the division between Heaven and Earth, began the separation between the different initial polarities: **Yang** (Heaven) and **Yin** (Earth), in the ancient oriental concept.

Man and the universe were divided: body and mind, masculine and feminine, active and passive, cold and hot, day and night, heavy and light, light and dark, beautiful and ugly, peaceful and aggressive, happy and sad, bad and good, among an infinite list whose main references are seen in The chart below. Everything has a Yin / Yang Characteristics.

YIN	YANG
Black	White
Even	Odd
Cold	Hot
Moon	Sun
Night	Day
Feminine	Masculine
Active	Passive
Concave	Convex
Internal	External
Soft	Hard
Horizontal	Vertical
2,4,6,8,10	1,3,5,7,9
Round	Angle
Earth	Heaven
Mountain	Sea
Small	High
Introverted	Extroverted

These two energies are in permanent interaction and its symbolism is represented by the division of the unity symbol - the circle - now replaced by the WAVE ... this wave, which still today, represents all forms of energy also generated by the interaction of two opposite poles - the positive and the negative.

Yin Yang, representation follow the traits representing the genitals of each of masculine and feminine sex, their essence: the positive and active Yang is represented by an arrow, a continuous movement to reach its target, as opposed to a Yin receptive and gradual movement represented by the broken line and the absorbing force.

A balanced environment needs a balance of all energies, taking into account the situation of the people living there, so you should pay attention to your surroundings, for example if you are someone with depressing tendencies (yin), you should balance your feng shui with some yang energy, like bright colors, sounds, energetic people, sports.

People's characteristics are also represented as the balance of this opposite forces, so we can analyze and balance our Social Support Network in what concerns their energies.

YANG - YIN : Big – Small, Strong – Weak, active – Passive, Wealth – Poverty, Extend - Retract

Energy is there since all ages, we are just rediscovering it

Invisible Energy is the "missing link" in the Universe, connecting the macro to microcosm, from the physical matter, to the subtle world of mental and neuro emotional connections. It is the "bridge" that connects all the worlds that we experience and surround, and at the same time is the vital force that animates our bodies.

Just imagine, you, seated in your room, alone, with nothing around you, just feeling the stillness and the peaceful sunset ..., suddenly you pick up your radio and the room fills with stereo rock music, you close it and get the GPS from your mobile phone and you can see satellite images of your far away office, and at the same time you connect your TV and you can see a live broadcast from Brazilian carnival.

Then you realize that you were not alone in the room, but instead you were surrounded by a sea of energy waves that you could not sense through your body decoders. When you get the right "decoder" you can sense and make sense of any specific type of energy, because of human limitations, there is a lot more that we can be in touch through our 5 senses, like the sub sonic sounds that only dogs can hear and not humans.

Our personal Yin / Yang, is reflected and reproduced in a basic survival mechanism, our Autonomic Nervous System (ANS). This "permanent commander" of our automatic responses, regulates all our main vegetative and vital systems like, digestion, breathing, eye movements even while we sleep.

ANS is an autonomous system, and at the slightest sign of danger - through memories kept for thousands of years in the limbic brain -, channels all our energy to "Fight or Fly", as an automatic reaction known as Caveman Reflex in detriment of the normal functioning of the body's self-regulating system. In modern society this is the bi-polarity "anxiety /depression".

We live, day to day, all of the waves that are currently present in our daily life: electric waves, tidal waves, emotional waves, radio waves, those of cell phones and TV's, the microwaves, the waves of fashion, the waves of each of our lives, with their fluctuations between different trends and extremes, and always with its cycle from beginning, growth and break, originating a new wave, in a perpetual and permanent dance between the highs and the lows.

"The existence and nonexistence produce each other;
The difficult and the easy complement each other;
The long and the short offset each other;
The high and the low incline towards each other;
Note and sound harmonize with each other;
Before and after follow each other."

Lao Tse

These extremes are all represented in the symbolism of Yin / Yang polarities that are present in every element of life. Even when we deal with numbers, we consider the odd numbers as Yang, and even numbers as Yin, the first being the luckiest ones; but once again the balance between them is considered to be the ultimate target, like for instance in the number of your house, or of your phone.

External an inner world are also mirrors of your reality, so Feng Shui connect and interacts with your internal states, from your surrounding energies, affecting your life through the perceptions of your minds, as it also look on how the impact of our micro facial emotional expressions of pain, joy, doubt, despise, or commitment, affect our partners and social relations.

The laws of YIN/YANG and the five elements

The philosophy of Yin / Yang is also used to describe things, people, situations, events, and even emotions. We can see the difference between discretion of a funeral (*Feng Shui Yin*), and the exuberance of a soccer game, clearly a *Yang* event; or the way how Yang anger, opposes Yin depression. In this case, someone who is very much Yin, with depressive tendencies, may get back its energy surrounded by a predominantly Yang environment.

Nothing is totally Yin or totally Yang.
In the midst of the greatest Yang, Yin is born,
in the deepest Yin, Yang is born...
as night becomes the day.

The ancient wisdom of a world of energy where there is a permanent interaction between all beings, things and situations, was rediscovered by western scientists the few decades in the begging of last century. This was called the new physics of quantum mechanics, dealing with Einstein's Nobel Prize equation, where matter equals energy $E=Mc2$, and ruled the world of the subatomic particles and speed higher then light.

Recent studies show that still today, more than 85% of health care in the world is based on traditional medicines, which mostly regard life balance, where humans, are the middle agent in the interplay between the heavenly or spiritual, and the earthly forces: the environment.

In personal Feng Shui, the Yin Yang represent the permanent interaction of these opposite forces, and they manifest in all surrounding people, things and situations, as we show you below.

Regarding the physical aspect, people with YANG characteristics, present a strong body and muscles, short and large hands and fingers, round head with small eyes and faces with sharp angles, while the YIN person will present round shapes, taller and thin body shape long fingers and large lips and eyes.

Emotions, will also define Yang personalities, with active, easily frustrated, enthusiastic, competitive, ambitious persons, and the YIN counterpart as insecure, depressive, sympathetic, peacefully, relaxed and hyper sensible emotional profiles.

Even food as its Yin Yang characteristics, where in the Yin side, we will find sugar, sweets, liquids, fruit and vegetables for the most commons, and in the Yang side, we find grains, meat, fish, salt, eggs, and most tubercles.

We finish this area summarizing the main laws regulating Yin and Yang which together with the energy quality and its quantity, are the basic stones of your Feng Shui.

- Yin Yang are connected and cannot exist one without another
- Yin and Yang are in a constant movement of change and balance as dynamic pairs of opposites
- Yin and Yang are not absolute but relative to each other
- In the deepest Yin emerges the Yang energy, and vice versa

- Yin and Yang create things in six stages layer by layer, as you will see in the chapter about I Ching Hexagrams.

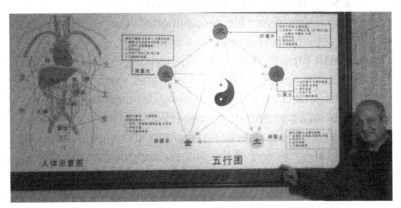

Fig3
The author in Chong Qing: China Interior City with drawings of five elements and the body Ba Gua

Five Elements to describe nature

The **Concept of the Five Elements** was developed to describe the cycles of Yin / Yang on Earth, and its relations to the 4 seasons, the 8 directions and trigrams and the natural phenomena:

> **Water** *yin*, with its peak in the winter, represented by the Northerly direction, and the deep spiritual insight on origins of life and feeds of the Wood in spring time.
> Stillness, calm, serenity, clarity of your thoughts, and the deep thinking and the gestation, the origin and birth of any process. Also used to raise the number of persons manifesting in your life.
> **Wood** grows to the East, feeding the Fire, and the huge energy of growth.
> Represent the growing phase of activity, vitality and the young and motivated energy of processes.

Fire *yang*, in the summit of summer, represented by the South where the sun warms the middle of the day, the energy in full expression, feeding the earth.

Expansion in your life, recognition of your merits, the peak of activity and energy of the process.

Earth growth from ashes generated by fire in the Fall/Autumn. In its interior it generates metal through the energetic contraction and consolidation of the energy

Stability, concentration, connection, and the slowing down, it is the phase of declining activity and energy of processes.

Metal is the end of the process and the consolidation of energy, together with the beginning of the renovation process. It melts into liquid, back into the Water frozen in winter under the ice.

Represents better communication, children's vitality and success; the cold energy of the contraction, end of the process, and the consolidation of the energy.

The Lunar calendar, integrates the 5 elements along the year, as wood growth in spring, fire in summer, metal in autumn, water in winter, within 72 days periods, and finally earth as an 18 days period between each season, so it completes 4 periods of 18 days in a total of 72 days also. It sums up the 360 days of the year calendar.

The Five Elements do not merely refer to Water, Wood, Fire, Earth, and Metal. The Chinese word for "element" means movement, change, or development. Each movement has its Yin and Yang aspect, and each should be in balance. A balanced environment, promotes peace and fortunate live.

Below you can find a chart mapping all the connections of the 5 elements which are the main tool to analyze and resolve imbalances of energy, from physical health to space acupuncture.

These five elements evolve within three cycles of relationships:

**the Production cycle,
the Control cycle, and
the Destruction cycle,**

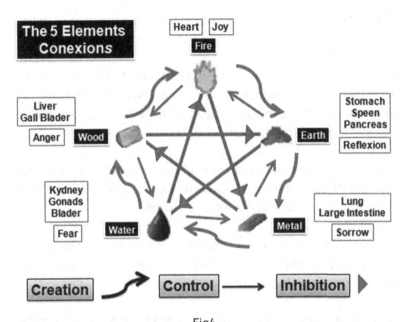

Fig4
The 5 Elements and their Creation, Control and Inhibition Cycles

Together, these cycles can be applied to every element on earth, to describe their relative situation, like for example, in the human body, reinforcing the Liver (wood element), to support the Heart (fire element).

In the case of Project Development by a company, it always starts with a brainstorm or any other type of thinking (metal), to develop the e-motions (water) to set the energies in motion, that increase the wood which is the symbol of the development and growth (of the project), until its consolidation (earth phase).

The *Production* cycle, as stated above, allow us to support one element that we lack of with the support of the previous element from this cycle.

Like water supports the wood, which feeds the fire with its ashes creates earth which hides the metal that melt into liquid water.

The *Control* cycle, allow us to slowly diminish the effect of an excessive element with its following element in the cycle, as when we play some metal music to activate one environment to excessively stable (earth element).

Water that erodes the metal emerging and controlling the land, where earth holds the fire, which burns and limits the wood growing in the forests, absorbing the excess of water.

Finally the *Destruction* cycle, allow us to counteract in a quick and strong way, the disturbing element, as when you put your hand under water if you burn your fingers.

In this cycle, water turns off fire, who melts the metal that cuts the wood with its roots tears the earth that contains the water.

When comparing with the occidental approach, the only element missing is the AIR, because in eastern vision, air is the FENG part of Feng Shui, so it is present everywhere, as CHI or vital energy.

The impact of the Season of Birth is essential, to understand how someone born with a specific element can present these characteristics in a more or less evident way. This is due to the strength of each element varying from season to season.

Earth prospers in all seasons because Earth is the transition element between any two Seasons, as for example, when Metal (Autumn) changes to Water (Winter) the transition element is Earth, hence the term "All Seasons" referring the last month (the third month) of every Season. For example, if a person is born in spring, then Wood prospers, Fire is born, Earth dies, Metal is imprisoned, and Water retreats.

Some connections of the five elements with their symbols, geographical directions, colors, shapes, sacred animals, and the human body are summarized below.

Wood (木)
Symbols: *Green plants, wood items, bamboo, rectangular shapes, lintel basketry*

> The East
> Spring time
> Dragon Azur
> The Planet Jupiter
> The Color Green
> Liver and Gall bladder

Fire (火)
Symbols: *Fires, candles, crystals, red roses*

> South
> Summer
> Red Phoenix
> The Planet Mars
> The Color Red
> Circulatory system & Heart & Small Intestine

Seasonal Cycle of the 5 Elements

Season	Elements				
	WATER	WOOD	FIRE	EARTH	METAL
Spring	Retreat	Prosper	Born	Die	Imprison
Summer	Imprison	Retreat	Prosper	Born	Die
Autumn	Born	Die	Imprison	Retreat	Prosper
Winter	Prosper	Born	Die	Imprison	Retreat
Between Seasons	Die	Imprison	Retreat	Prosper	Born

Fig 5

Earth (土)
Symbols: *Stoneware, pot plants, statues, sun flowers*

Centre
Between seasons (the last month of the season)
Yellow Dragon
The Planet Saturn
The Color Yellow
Rat
Digestive system, Spleen and Stomach

Metal (金)
Symbols: *Wind chimes, silver vases, brass bolls, candle sticks*

West
Autumn
White Tiger
Planet Venus
Color White
Respiratory system & Lung & Large Intestine

Water (水)
Symbols: Aquariums, fountains, ponds, glassware

North
Winter
Black Tortoise
Planet Mercury
Color Black
Skeleton, Urinary Bladder & Kidney

In the following map, you can see the main characteristics of the elements you can use, to enhance each Feng Shui "cure" based on the elements.

⊕	ELEMENTS and Their Associations				
	Water	Wood	Fire	Earth	Metal
Direction	North	W / SW	South	SE / NW	E / NE
Season	Winter	Spring	Summer	End of Season	Autumn
Energy	Coldness	Wind	Heat	Dampness	Dryness
Taste	Salty	Sour	Bitter	Sweet	Pungent Hot
5 Senses	Ears	Eyes	Tongue	Mouth	Nose
Emotion	Fear	Anger	Happiness	Reflexion	Melancholy
Organ Yin	Kidney	Liver	Heart	Spleen	Lungs
Organ Yang	Bladder	Gall Blader	Small Intestine	Stomach	Large Intestine
Tissues	Tendons	Vessels	Muscles	Skin - Hair	Bones
Color	Black	Green	Red	Yellow	White
Sounds	Pour	Shout	Laugh	Sing	Cry
Grains	Soybean	Wheat	Rice	Corn	Oat
Basic Shapes					
Planet	Mercury	Jupiter	Mars	Saturn	Venus

Fig 6
Five Elements their characteristics and balancing solutions

The use of the five elements is among the most important remedies to balance the Feng Shui of a place, affecting the Chi. In order to enhance each one of the missing elements in a building you must choose the symbols of that element or the one that creates it within the production cycle.

For example, to enhance the wood element you would choose to put some green plants with some rectangular or bamboo shapes, or you could use the water influence through a cascade, a fountain or even a painting with water scenarios.

Man, Heaven and Earth, the Trigrams and Ba GUA

Trigrams appeared as a way to represent the relations of Man as the link between heaven and earth. When you consider the Yin Yang energies represented by the broken and continuous lines, mathematically there are only eight possibilities of combining Yin ▬ ▬ and Yang ▬▬▬ on trigrams, or combinations of three lines.

Each trigram, with its three lines represents a specific relationship of Man as a mediator between Heaven and Earth:

Fu Xi (5.000 BC), the original creator of the Trigrams and later the Hexagrams of the "Y Jing" or I Ching, first duplicated the two lines to create the 4 Images Supreme Yang and Young Yang, opposed to the Supreme Yin and the Young Yin.

The 8 trigrams are the result of these combinations, and each one represents a natural phenomenon. Their complete set of possible combinations generate the 64 hexagrams the I Ching - the Book of Changes -, whose origin, lost in the mists of time is estimated at also around 5,000 years BC, and will be explored further in part III of this book.

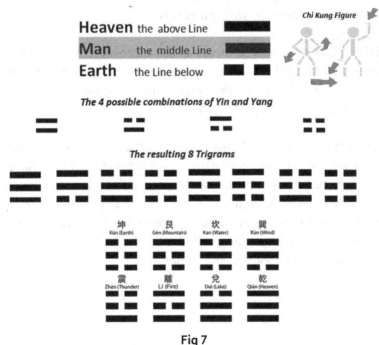

Fig 7
Man between Heaven and Earth
The 8 Trigrams and the natural phenomena they represent

Trigrams are the inner code of the main reference book from eastern philosophy, adopted and enriched by all major masters from east and west, Lao Tse, to Confucius, and even by Carl Jung. It contains the basic wisdom of the universe and is connected with all its major driving forces.

Trigrams contain paired opposite forces that are clearly pictured when presented in the following organization of each pair of trigrams:

> *Earth and Heaven, the pure energy and its material condensation*
> *Mountain and Lake, the solid and the liquid*
> *Water and Fire, emotion and action*
> *Wind and Thunder, strong and soft*

The eight trigrams as a summary of the expression of the natural forces on a 3D world, mediated by men, are the origin of the two sequences of their arrangement expressing the heaven and earthly matters, called Ba Gua or Pa Kua,.

Ba Gua the Chinese word for 8 trigrams is the diagram expressing the interaction of the main natural phenomena, and they have two proposed sequences representing two different perspectives: The **Early Heaven Ba Gua** with the organization of pure heavenly energy, or the **Later Heaven Pa Gua,** resulting from their earthly expression, when interacting with the 4 seasons, the 5 elements, and the natural phenomena they represent.

Nr. KUA or TRIGRAM	1 乾 Qián (Heaven)	2 兌 Dui (Lake)	3 離 Li (Fire)	4 震 Zhèn (Thunder)	5 巽 Xun (Wind)	6 坎 Kan (Water)	7 艮 Gèn (Mountain)	8 坤 Kun (Earth)
Nature	Heaven	Lake	Fire	Thunder	Wind	Water	Mountain	Earth
Name	CHIEN	TUI	LI	CHEN	SUN	KAN	KEN	KUN
Element	Metal	Metal	Fire	Wood	Wood	Water	Earth	Earth
Concept	Creator	Serenity	Adherent	Promoting	Penetrating	Abyss	Imobiling	Receiver
Direction	SW	W	S	E	SE	N	NE	NW
Color	WHITE/GOLD	WHITE/GOLD	RED/PURPLE	GREEN	GREEN/PURPLE	BLACK	BEIJE	TERRACOTA
Months	October	Aug.-Sept.	May.-June	March-April	April-May	Nov.-Dic.-Jan.	January.-Feb.	June-July
Body	Head	Mouse-Tongue	Eyes	Foot	Legs	Ears-Heart	Nose-Spleen Hands	Belly
Family	Father-Brother	Younger Daughter	Middle Daughter	Older Son	Older Daughter	Middle Son	Younger Son	Mother Sister
Social	Noble Man	Young woman	Middle age woman	Merchant-Middle Age Woman	Adult Man age (30-45 years)	Young Adult age (20-35 years)	Young Man age (17-25 years)	People's Man Woman
Symbolic	Noble protector, Assisting People, Travel, Cold, Ice	Lover, Neigbour, Satisfaction, Magic, Chilfren, Offspring	Fame, Sun, Dry, Soldier, Student	Expansion, road, lightning, Familly	Attack-Withdraw, Hesitation, Wealth, Work	Foundation, Career, Falling, Driver, Hidden, Occult	Knowledge, Studies, Employee, Dwarf, Cat, Dog	Marriage, Partnerships, Economy, Farmer, Multitude
Animal	DOG-PIG	ROOSTER	HORSE	RABBIT	DRAGON-SNAKE	RAT	OX	SHEEP

TRIGRAMS (KUA) and their CONECTIONS

Fig 8

The eight Trigrams their sequences and characteristics

The Early Heaven BA GUA

This primal heavenly arrangement of the 8 Trigrams or BA Gua, created by the Emperor FU XI, represents the pure form of energy from heaven, and its natural movement. Its usage is intended mainly as a protection symbol for energetic Feng Shui remedies.

This sequence represents the hereditary forces and our psycho-genealogy, that where already present at the moment of birth together with the new coming energies from respiratory and digestive systems.

The Later Heaven BA GUA

The Later Heaven Sequence, is due to King WEN, The Trigrams are arranged based on their connection to the nature cycles of the seasons and the five elements,and is used for work in space ergonomics', organization and acupuncture, what is called Feng Shui for the Livings, and it is what we use as a map, to analyze and organize the areas (Mansions) of our life Feng Shui.

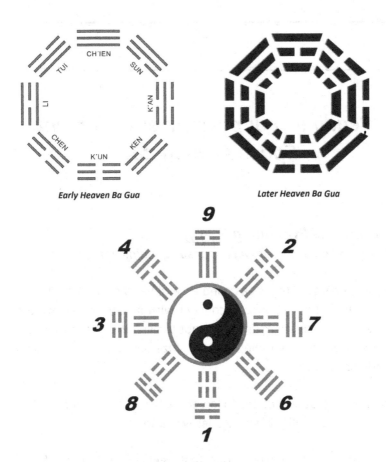

Early Heaven Ba Gua

Later Heaven Ba Gua

Later Heaven BA GUA

NR.	TRIGRAM	Nature	Element	Mouvement
9	Li	Fire	Fire	Push
2	KUN	Earth	Earth	Reverse
7	TUEI	Lake	Metal	Test your strenght
6	CHIEN	Heaven	Metal	Repulse
1	KAN	Water	Water	Press
8	KEN	Mountain	Earth	Shoulder Press
3	ZHEN	Thunder	Wood	Split
4	SUEN	Wind	Wood	Launch

Fig 9
Ba Gua or the original sequences of the eight Trigrams

2

Reading your physical environment Space Acupuncture

Sensing and Evaluating Energy
Identify, change and amplify your surrounding energies

Sensing energy (Chi), is easy and accessible to everybody. We all have this Chi! So we all can connect with it. Off course, we are more sensible to energies we are not familiar with because when we get used to something we desensitize our perception to avoid overloading.

This means that we need to follow some few rules in order to allow us to raise our ability to sense energy in a space.

First you need to trust your first feelings, because of the desensitation process, and if you did not perceived the energy at first, you probably will not get it the second time.

Use the natural, meaning that you should look around to the natural environment and try to get the most information from it. You can use cats, seating on the bad energy, or Dogs, looking for the best spots, or even looking at birds and plants where they are stronger and healthy.

Start to understand what you feel before entering the space, then move into it and feel the difference. Now believe your senses and feelings, because everything in a place affects you, like colors, shapes, things, and even the internal organization of it.

Look at what calls first for your attention. Usually it is the more energetic spot. Pay attention if this spot is outside the building, like a nice green forest... energy will also, probably, try to escape from the house attracted to the garden, but you need to keep it inside, so maybe you could use some interior plants, even artificial ones.

The Yin / Yang energy is the first to notice and should be the first to balance. Every situation is a blend of energies that are more or less suitable depending on the subject and its intentions. This is why all "out of context" evaluation is nonsense.

For example, the location for the bed, in a bedroom of a couple, needs a very different energy and settings, if we deal with a young couple just married, more like the area 7 of the Ba Gua as we will see later, or a stable long lasting relation, more suitable in area 3 of the Ba Gua.

It is through the identification and evaluation of the different types of energy, in relation to their quantities and qualities, that we can define the existing imbalances and therefore reorganize the environment to counteract energetic deficiencies and excesses.

Find below, several types of energy, you may find in different locations, with their opposite qualities,

Tranquil	Restless
Relaxed	Tense
Friendly	Indifferent
Emotional	Thoughtful
Formal	Informal
Interior	Exterior

Together with the Quality of the energy present, you should also evaluate their Quantity, using for instance, a scale from 0 to 10, so we will have a full evaluation and its measure, the only way that allow us acting over it, and monitor the changes afterwards.

Actually we have available on the market devices that can measure energies in a very quick and effective way, from very small ranges of ELF (Extremely Low Frequencies) to High frequencies, that evaluate EMF (Electro Magnetic Fields) pollution from earth known as Geopathology.

EXERCISE: *Sensing Energies*

Take a tour outside and clear your mind of internal talk, taking some deep breaths, counting to 4 each time .... in .... hold .... out .... hold .... with your eyes closed, and at the same time focusing in a Big golden star in the middle of your eyebrows.

Now go to your living room, close your eyes at the entrance...inhale and exhale lengthily... open your eyes after that... See, listen, feel...

Analyze now the type and quality of energy (Chi) of this space...

What kinds of energy can you identify in each space?

How is the balance between them?

Being aware of these subtle energies is the foundation of a conscious co-creation of a wonderful life through the path of least resistance.

The Art of Location
The perfect location and the four sacred animals

Remembering an ancient armchair, with a strong stable back and to arms at each side, with an open view to the front, that is the modern view of the perfect location of a place referred to the four sacred animals, the Turtle, the Dragon, the Tiger and the Phoenix.

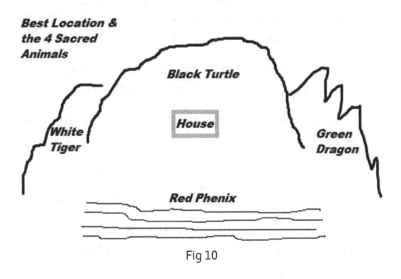

Fig 10

In the East, it is the Blue-Green Dragon. In the West, it is the White Tiger. In the North, it is the Black Turtle. In the South, it is the Red Bird Phoenix.

The Black Turtle longevity and stability, protecting the back, as the mountains protect china from northern attacks, the Green Dragon, with sharp mountain picks protecting the east, and the White Tiger smooth mountains protecting west winds, surrounding an open view to the south where the sun comes from and there should be the Red Phoenix, opening the smooth road to a permanent renewed and bright future, symbolized by a peaceful moving water.

Preliminary and general tips for shapes and locations of land and buildings

To evaluate the potential of any property, you should first consider its environment, namely using the checklist below.

> History of the property: avoid buying buildings that were sold or abandoned by people in needing situations, and look for those new, or sold by people that moved away improving their situation in life

> The building should not be lower than its neighbors but lower than those behind it, for the protection of the black turtle.

> Regular shapes as squares and rectangles are most suitable and balanced

> The left and right portion of the land should be balanced

> Avoid a property with a building with water in behind

> Water fountains, waterfalls, even artificial created, in the garden, will improve the Feng Shui of the place

> Finally you should check about the Geobiology of the house: the "Dragon Veins", and ovoid to place your sofas, chairs, and other stable places over this lines or worst their crossing points.

Geobiology is the science that studies the natural energetic networks crossing the planet, namely the "Telluric currents network" which are energetic beams crossing the earth with specific natural radioactivity that you can measure even at the top of the highest buildings.

There exists many types of these telluric currents that are phenomena observed in the Earth's crust and mantle, but the main two networks, are the Hartmann and the Curry, named after the geologists that discovered them.

Ley lines are man-made energy lines, created by stone formations such as Stonehenge or other ancient archaeological structures. Ley lines are alleged alignments of a number of places of geographical interest, such as ancient monuments and megaliths that are thought to have spiritual power.

Using Cats and Dogs to find these hot locations is a natural and very inexpensive way to find your best and worst spots, instead of and expert: Dogs will look for good energy, and cats will be seated in the worst energy places. You can also use them to identify the best and worst energy places in your house.

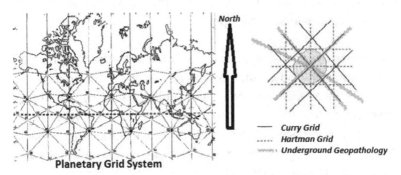

Planetary Grid System

North

——— *Curry Grid*
..... *Hartman Grid*
⌇⌇⌇ *Underground Geopathology*

Fig 11
Planetary Global Energy Networks and their directions

The Hartmann or Global network, is oriented exactly around the cardinal points is composed by lines oriented North/South 2 meters apart, and lines oriented East/West, 2,5 meters apart, their width being around 20 cm in normal conditions. Their neutral zone is located in the center.

The effects, in humans and animals or plants of this network are connected with the line involved, and the most affected areas are over their crossing points.

The N/S lines are charged with Yin energy, slow and cold, corresponding to winter, and so originating all sorts of humidity effects like in rheumatism and cramps. The E/W lines have a Yang energy and are responsible by inflammations and infections, due to their fire characteristics of hot, high speed and dryness.

The Curry or Diagonal network, is oriented in diagonal related to the previous one, and the hot lines are oriented NW/SE and NE/SW, this latest being a very strong energy one, found in several cathedrals around the world. Curry lines are approximately 3 meters apart (with variations), diagonally to the poles, east to west.

A **"Star Point"**, is where a superposition of two crossings of a Hartmann and a Curry line occur, and they should be absolutely avoided to place any human spot.

Water was used since all ages to reinforce or hinder the physical or the spiritual body. Small or large streams and brooks cross under Dolmens Menhirs and other buildings made by ancestors, the churches and cathedrals, where we can detect the water flows located in very specific places, to reinforce one or the other bodies. This is done through the electric currents in the streams that's are proportional to their speed and volume.

Also the energies carried by this waters, depend on their course, like pure rocks charged with minerals, underground or surface waters, or in the opposite end crossing cemeteries, cities, or waste disposals. These water streams, can impact or health, together with your wellness.

The interior design

Acupuncture of the space

Acupuncture is another area of traditional Chinese medicine that only recently has been enthusiastically welcomed and validated in the Western countries.

Similar to the Acupuncture channels in the human body - the 12 meridians -, the work of Feng Shui is done through the "acupuncture of space."

The Synchronic lines on earth correspond to the meridians of the planet Earth, of which they cover circumferentially near the surface, around 15m below, from one side to the other are already known, since ancient times. Emperors made their annual prayers in "acupuncture points" of their empires, as for example, the Summer Palace in Beijing, China, or the stone next to Red Square in Moscow, Russia, we can see in the picture.

Similarly, the work of Feng Shui in the interior of the spaces is carried out using an analysis grid called Lo Shu, organized in 9 Mansions representing the nine areas of life, also connected to the five traditional elements.

The Magic Square was first mentioned in the Legend of the River "Lo", from where a sacred path in a turtle shell originate the Book of "Lo" or Lo Shu, and is the origin of the Ba Gua, that associates each Gua (or trigram) possessing certain characteristics, with the numbers of the Chinese numerology of the I Ching.

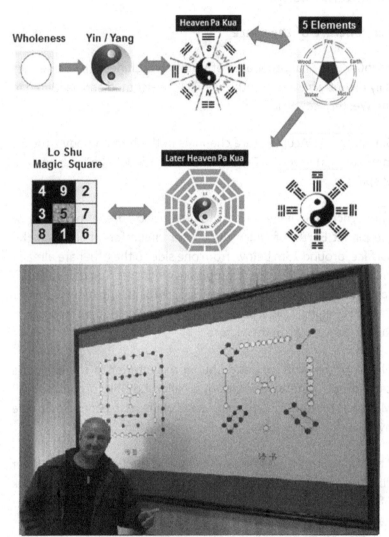

Wholeness   Yin / Yang

Heaven Pa Kua

5 Elements

Lo Shu
Magic Square

Later Heaven Pa Kua

The author in Chongqing with paintings representing the original Lo Shu from the Yellow River Turtle marks.

Fig 12
The author and a painting of the original drawings of the Lo Shu from the legend of the Book of Lo, in ChongQing inner China

This "Lo Shu" is actually a Mandala, integrating a huge accumulation of knowledge from centuries of observation and mathematical studies, under the apparent simplicity of a square with nine numbers, it covers the secret of a full cosmological approach with a perfect mathematical coherence, and the bi-dimensional spiral representation of the atmospheric flow of Chi.

Basic 'Lo Shu' Square

4 Wood	9 Fire	2 Earth
3 Wood	5 Earth	7 Metal
8 Earth	1 Water	6 Metal

Characteristics of each Lo Shu area

4 Power Abundance	9 Image Projection Spiritual alignment Self-knowledge Projects	2 Relationships Partners, Associates,
3 Bases (Origins) Nuclear Family Psycho Genealogy	5 Health Primary Energy of Space	7 Creativity Children
8 Studies, Spirituality Learning	1 Career Life Project/Goals Way of life	6 Friends, Protectors Helpful People Traveling

Fig 13
Working diagram with the Magic Square and the Ba Gua

In the Ba Gua octagon, the eight directions are represented associated with eight basic trigrams from the I Ching as well as the five elements. This is the basic matrix where have been located the areas of life presented in the magic square, or the practical diagram of work, presented in Fig 13.

In this Basic Matrix with 3 rows and 3 columns defining 9 spaces, there are 8 sequences of 3 numbers, including 2 diagonals. Adding up all the numbers of each line the result is always the number 15. This is the basic tool to, implement effective Feng Shui work at your place.

From this basic matrix (3 X 3), we can mathematically upgrade it to a superior level, from 9 numbers to 81, to generate a 9 X 9 **Matrix 81** of a more detailed magic Square through a secret formula.

First we design the New Matrix 81, dividing each one of the nine areas of the original Lo Shu, into 9 other similar spaces creating the basic 9 X 9 structure. In this new Major Matrix, Now place each of the nine numbers in it's original position within the number 1 case of each area.

Now we will fill this Matrix 81, with the next level of 9 numbers from 10 to 18, and we place them in the House corresponding to number 2 in the original magic square. Next level with numbers from 19 to 27 will be placed in the House corresponding to number 3, and so on until the level 9 with numbers from 73 to 81, are placed in the House number 9.

All the secret potential of information from this huge matrix is still unveiled but we can already, check some mathematical features of it, like the sum of the digits of any number of a house it repeats the Ruler Number of that same House. For example in house number **9** you can check 81= (8 + 1) = **9**, 45= (4 + 5)= **9**, or in House **3** were 39= (3 + 9)=12 (1 + 2)= **3**, 48= (4 + 8)= 12 (1 + 2)= **3**

31	76	13	36	81	18	29	74	11
22	40	58	27	45	63	20	38	56
67	4	49	72	9	54	65	2	47
30	75	12	32	77	14	34	79	16
21	39	57	23	41	59	25	43	61
66	3	48	68	5	50	70	7	52
35	80	17	28	73	10	33	78	15
26	44	62	19	37	55	24	42	60
71	8	53	64	1	46	69	6	51

Fig 14
The Lo Shu amplified

The sum of all numbers in any row including the diagonals add up to 369, dividing 369 / 9 = **41** which is the central number of the whole matrix, and its complexity growths like the Mayan or Aztec Calendars, namely to calculate exactly the years, months and agricultural nature rhythms.

Key rules to analyze and activate your house Ba Gua

Feng Shui and how to set the environment to support your targets, is connected with the perception of our energy and of the energies that surround us in an innovative, original and target oriented perspective.

The organization of the inner spaces, takes increasing and utmost importance, because nowadays, is difficult to analyze beforehand, the external environment and relative positioning of our living and work places, as well as the energies involved, when most of the time, buildings and apartments are already-built, without our opinion, influence or the proper guidelines for construction, due to the whole lot of other external variables.

Feng Shui of the EXTERIOR deals with the outer forms and location, as well as the Feng Shui of the INTERIOR deals in addition to the main energy of the space, also with the relative position of the different rooms, and the internal organization, evaluated through the floor plan of the building, with a specific emphasis in the following areas:

Circulation of the Chi
Yin/Yang balance
Main door
Bedrooms
Living room
Dining room
Kitchen
Bathrooms
Office
Beams
Stairways

Some common rules of the main Feng Shui approach are,

- We identify the situation, then remove any hindrance, so first we eliminate all unnecessary clutter, later we harmonize and create the energy needed in one's life.
- This task is performed in each space and areas of a house, using, the Feng Shui "cures" every time you need it.
- The relative situation of everything, is dominant in relation to its absolute positioning, which means that to optimize the magnetic directions, we should first regard for the relative position of all objects.

The 3 doors Ba Gua

The Ba Gua Matrix and the LO SHU Square, are the frame for the structure of analysis of each space, room or entire building or location.

First you should draw a map of the location and then design a Square or a Rectangle covering it, using the largest side as a basis for the outline.

Then you need to devise each side in three equal parts to get nine areas of equal size, each one corresponding to a functional area of life, thus creating the internal Ba Gua of that specific space, as seen on the figure below.

Following, we look at the entrance door and its main line, where are the areas 8, 1 and 6. The location of the entrance door in each of the areas tells us what is the main orientation of that room or building. It can be the 8th Mansion for Knowledge, study and learning, the 1srt Mansion for career, profession or life prospects, or the 6th mansion for friends, protectors, mentors and outside helpers, as we can see below.

The next step is to identify the different LO SHU areas and their specific characteristics as we will show hereafter.

The line with the numbers 8, 1, 6, is placed aligned with the front door and, depending on the location of this door; in each of the numbers, we have a different basic Chi or vocational energy of this house or room:

Depending on the entrance door which defines the essence of the room, you may have: 8 for Knowledge, 1 for Career or 6 for Mentors, the energy will flow to the extreme opposite of the entrance area, creating what is called the "Power or Control area", of the room.

3 Doors Ba Gua

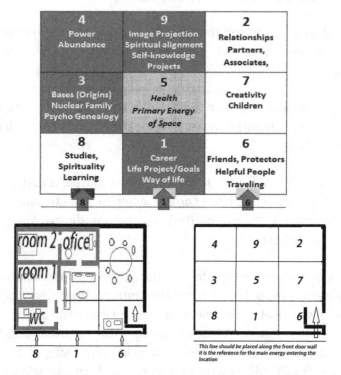

Fig 15
**The line is to be positioned aligned to the front door wall
reflecting the 3 possible Door locations (8, 1, or 6)**

EXERCISE

- Draw the map of the room you select, as a square or a rectangle
- Divide each side by 3 to design the LO SHU over the place.
- Align the side of the wall where is the entrance door with the side of the Ba Gua numbers 8, 1 and 6
- Check and locate the entrance door and evaluate the following questions:

1- what is the entrance energy? Knowledge, Career or Mentorship?

2- Where is the "command area" of the room and what energy it represents?

The access to your entrance door, together with the first room you see when you enter the house is a key issue to the appropriate Feng Shui for wealth and success.

There are some rules for auspicious and inauspicious access passages to your location that you may find below.

Auspicious passages to access your front door:

- A winding path or walkway
- A circular path or walkway
- A broad path or walkway

Inauspicious passages to access your front door:

- A straight path or walkway
- Sharp angled path or walkway
- A narrow path or walkway
- A major overwhelming object in front of your main entrance door

The secrets of the Life Mansions

Put the Ba Gua map over the floor plan of your house, stretching the sides in order to fit them to the external walls.

Now identify what fits in what area of the Ba Gua: rooms and their inhabitants, bathrooms and its energetic drains, work areas, study areas, leisure areas, play areas, etc.

Check the GUA (trigram) energy of each room, and its location in each of the areas of the Ba Gua.

Are these the energies that you pretend, in each of these specific areas?

EXERCISE: *analyze de full house*

From the Magic Square that has already been placed on the floor plan of your house, in the previous exercise:

1. mark and identify each one of the zones and get the first contact with your energetic diagram and the subtle meanings from the location function of each mansion described on the Fig 16.
2. now analyze the intensity and the quality of each of these areas of life, adjust or correct their energy to suit your goals and needs. To do so, you may apply the "Feng Shui remedies presented below, to each of these interior spaces.

EXERCISE: *analyze each room*

1. Start by visiting each of these rooms, close your eyes at the entrance...inhale and exhale lengthily... open your eyes after that... See, listen, feel...
2. Analyze now the type and quality of energy (Chi) of this space... (Please refer to the graphic on Qualities of the Energy we mentioned before).
   Does it show more *Yin* or more *Yang* and where is any of them providing more "action" or "rest"? Do you have a more "fun" or "industrious" Chi? Is the area more "emotional" or more "intellectual"? Is it more "physical" or more "spiritual"? What other kinds of energy can you identify in each space?

3. Now you may check ... Is this the most appropriate energy to achieve my goals?

Case Study about a House analysis

You may find in the Fig 15, one house and the superposition of the Ba Gua Matrix over it, with its numbers to allow an easy location of every specific area, and main furniture.

When you evaluate the house below, you should start from its environmental localization followed by the analysis of the main entrance door, as the Chi entrance gate.

In this case you find a Phenomena called "Hidden Door" which is a door opening 90 degrees from the main entrance wall. This door creates two main problems:

1. one is that this phenomena means loosen opportunities, so you may miss several chances in life,
2. the second is that it creates a missing space in area 6 of the Ba Gua representing mentors, and helpers, so you may feel a lack of supportive people to help you progress in that level.
This is of outmost importance when this area is where is located the Kitchen and the stove, meaning the production of abundance, so you may lack of income also.

This door shows also the entrance of the 3 doors Ba Gua representing mentors and helpers, in area 6, so this will set the main energy of this house to highlight and reinforce this domain of your life, and balancing the "hidden door phenomena" in this case.

Finally, checking the general energy flow, there are not main obstacles to a free flow in the main rooms, except in area 6, behind the door where is the kitchen, where a dead corner needs to be activated to avoid stagnant energy there.

Looking at each room location you find out that there is a toilet with its drains exactly on the spirituality and knowledge area meaning that all your knowledge may be lost. The resting and working rooms are well placed in the inner posterior part 4 and 9, the dining room is covering the corners of relations and creativity 2 and 7. Central area 5, is where you seat and relax with family and friends. Finally your office is well located in area 9 of fire and image.

Now you enter the house and check every room, detect any problems and evaluate how to apply the solutions we propose below.

In room 1 we find that the bed is located with the head towards the wall of the WC which will drain all energy during the night, and you may feel tired in the morning, besides with this position the person cannot see naturally the entrance door of the room. The room 2 well balanced and the desk office is in the power position related to the main entrance door.

EXERCISE: *Feng Shui Solutions for your house*

Based on the example above, and the solutions that follow in the next chapters, you should check and find solutions for the main issues concerning your house, namely:

Entrance door
Dead corner
Toilet
Bed in room 1
Abundance
Friends and helpers reinforcement

3

Basic rules to feng shui your home and office

From the general location, to the internal environment of your building

Internal environment

After analyzing your location surroundings, you should check the building and its inside. This is the main target of Feng Shui of interiors.

- The main door should be strong and solid
- Windows should not be bigger than the door except if they have several crystal squares
- Windows are better if they open out then sliding ones
- The main door should be bigger than the back door
- The living room should be well lit
- Avoid sofas with "L" shape
- Use tall plants to enhance stagnant energy from protruding corners
- Avoid Dark blue for walls of the rooms
- Earth colors like yellow and terracotta are good for the bathroom
- Use soft tones in the bedrooms
- Round tables are better for dinning
- Dining rooms should be the center or deep inside the house
- Bathrooms should be far from the kitchen

- Bathrooms doors should be closed at all times
- The "power spot" of every room is located in the opposite corner of the entrance door
- Balance the elements on each room with shapes, colors, materials, tools
- Check the symbolic decoration of each room
- Sense if the energy is the most suitable for its purpose

The bed and the office desk

- Separate sleeping and working areas
- All ways sleep with a solid wall behind the bed
- Avoid a mirror facing the bed (even a Tv or Pc screen)
- The bed should not face the door (check the power spot of the room)
- Always keep your desk supported by a a solid wall

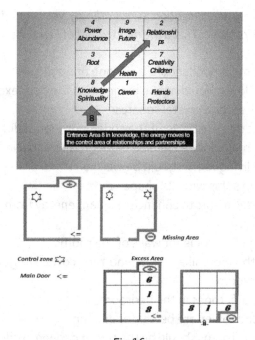

Fig 16
Energy flow, control zone, excess and deficient areas in house

Feng Shui General Solutions

There are several solutions that help to enhance or balance the energy of any location disregarding its space relationships. These are usually called Feng Shui "cures", and use the different formulas of the Yin Yang energy, the five elements, the Trigrams and directions, the energy quality and quantity, as tools to act and modify space energies.

You may start, after sensing the main global energy of the space, by identifying the general issues that promote or enhance a supportive Chi, or in the other hand bring bad energy into a space, like the following things and situations.

- Space where energy can easily flow not messed up
- Harmonic combination of elements in the production cycle
- Illumination
- Cleanness
- Flavors and fragrances
- Healthy plants (even artificial ones can improve the energy)
- Healthy animals
- Sound and music
- Water fountains
- Colorful flowers
- Stones
- Parties with friends
- Sharp corners of columns, furniture, external buildings, project sharp energy that can hinder the areas it crosses
- Dead angles accumulate dead energy
- Objects associated with bad or inconvenient memories

The Yin and Yang balance, impact heavily our mood and usually a well-balanced yin yang environment is more suitable, except in situations with specific unbalances of the inhabitants, like depression where they will need a more yang energy, or hyperactivity where a Yin environment would be recommended.

So this balance is the next evaluation you should check, using also an objective approach, through their relevant characteristics like,

For the **Yin** side,

Lower sofas and chairs, curves and round shapes, horizontal, low light, paintings and decoration motifs, smooth colors, walls with spaces, calm, sand, low sounds and tranquil moods. Also the rooms in the back of the property are more Yin and appropriated for relax and rest.

For the **Yang** side,

Sharp and geometrical shapes, strong lights, arm chairs and sofas, vertical and high motifs, bright colors, ceramics and bricks, walls full of things, nude space, minimalist. The action rooms are the working areas, the kitchen, or even the seating room.

Next you should look at the five elements harmony, which can be identified through all their connections like shapes and symbols, and they should be all present in a balance that may compensate any previous natural deficit of the place.

For this purpose you can either use the specific element characteristics or those of the element that helps it regarding the production cycle. For example if you need fire, you can use either red color (fire), or the Green color for Wood element that will produce fire according to the natural way of the five elements.

Solutions for each elements can use different associated things to each element as we show you below,

Fire element
Colors red, purple, dark orange and pink
Triangles, pyramids and sharp shapes
All light sources such as candles, sunshine, fireplaces, matches, lights
Pets, and all art figures representing people or animals
Number 9

Earth element
Colors brown, yellow, terracotta
Square and large curves shapes
Bricks, ceramic's, tiles, clay stuff
Symbols and pictures showing mountains and fields
Numbers 2, 5, 8

Metal element
Colors white and silver
Domes, circles, arches, sphere shapes
Metal objects in any form, from noble metals to daily pieces
Marble, rocks, slabs, granite
Computers, TV's, communication and sound systems
Numbers 6 and 7

Water element
Black and dark blue colors
Wave and asymmetrical shapes with free flowing
Crystals, mirrors, all reflecting surfaces
Water fountains, reservoirs, sinks, taps

Wood element
Any green color
Columns, rectangles, stripes, pedestals
Wood furniture, plants, flowers, all plant base tissues
All objects and art representing gardens, trees, flowers

Specific Solutions and their particularities

Some specific solutions are more commonly applied, but they need some more careful approach. Every solution should be connected with an intention clearly expressed. You can see how to well define an objective in the last part of the book. The full list of remedies with the respective intention in written form is a exceptional map of your shui cure and monitoring.

You can find a list of the most important below.

Mirrors

These are called the Feng Shui aspirin, because of their versatility and wide usage. A good mirror should be clean and distortion free, without being broken or cracked, because any distortion of the person image can disrupt its energy.

They can be used mostly to erase an area, like when you put them in a wall of the bath room to eliminate its effect, or to slow or accelerate the energy, like when you put it in a wall in the middle of a corridor or in the middle of huge stairs, or to protect the place, as when put in front of the entrance door to send back the incoming energy.

Mirrors should be one only piece and placed at the eyes height of the highest person in the house, disregarded of their dimensions. They can attract and make energy flow slower than in straight line.

Also, a mirror on the door facing a very busy avenue or an overbearing building, will send back the excessive Chi.

Finally they are also used to bring into the room or into that area, some surrounding energy, like when it reflects the green trees of the external garden into the room, bringing a fresh wood energy of expansion.

Colors

Adapt the colors to the function and energy you wish for every area, according to its location in the Ba Gua, the elements, the Yin Yang and your personal taste.

To bring all of the five elements in a room only based in colors you can choose for instance, the ceiling painted in white (metal), with walls in beige (earth), one green carpet (wood), with red sofa (fire) together with a blue marine wall.

You can also use colors to specific usages like the peach to bring up more lovely relations to your life, but do not forget to change them once you get what you want, or it will keep rolling on.... Also dim and pastel colors smooth the energy, while bright colors enhance the same energy.

Candles and lights

They promote the Fire element, and should be used with caution. Soft and subtle lights are relaxing and bring good fortune, when too bright and glaring have the opposite effect, and may hurt your eyes.

Candles are used to harmonize the energy in rooms irregularly shaped, and are good also to brighten dark corners or dim spots.

Sound

Energy is based on wave frequencies, so the sound and its quality is an important element of the room energy. Either low or high, heavy metal or classic music, water fountains, or birds singing, traffic jams

J.J. Lupi

honking, wind chimes, will bring a very different energy flow and quality to any location.

A pleasant sound have a huge effect on every space and its occupants. Also every word and the tone of your conversations are a part of the local energy, so beware of what and how you speak.

Lights

Light can be natural or artificial, candles, light bulbs, can enrich and raise the energy of a stagnant area or room.

Dark areas accumulate bad and stagnant energy, and need to be activated, for which light and bright moving colors are very effective.

Wind Chimes and bells, will energize the metal or wood element and connect with the wind and bring the Chi into the room or the house. Usually you hang them near the entrance or a window.

Crystals

They enhance the earth element, disperse into small portions and activate light helping to spread its influence into the room.

They also have specific properties and energy, and can be charged and retain energy because of their crystalline structure.

It is particularly auspicious to hang a glass ball reflecting the rays of the morning sun.

Incense

Used mostly to clean the space is called "the Rain". You should use it to catch the bad energy of the space with the smog. To use it, you should walk with it through the room with the windows closed, and only after you will open the windows, so it takes away the energy collapsed with the smog.

The side or main effect is also the fragrance impact on the human. The sense of smell affects the brain area that regulates emotions, so you can have a major impact on your mood using the adequate flavor.

Living plants

They energize the element wood, and are good to brighten dark corners or dim spots, on your living or dining room. Avoid to use them in the kitchen or bed room.

Be sure to take care of them so they keep healthy and robust. If you can't is better to use artificial ones.

Aquariums

Enhance the water energy, and it attracts Chi, wealth and prosperity, even with a single fish ball.

If you cannot take good care of a live aquarium, you may use alternatives like paintings or photos with water subjects, aiming to compensate a lack of "sea view" in your house.

Art, stones and heavy objects

Used to reinforce earth element, and can also deviate energy to slow it down, and they can fix and stabilize the energy in Ba Gua areas that present some instability.

Together with ceramic vases, and pots, big aquariums and fountains circulate the money (water is money), round tables, they activate the energy, wealth and promote the circulation of the Chi.

Symbols have always play an important role in energy, since all ages. So beware of what is the symbolic meaning of everything you have in your personal space.

Where does it comes from?
What does it means to me?
What energy it brings?

Symbolic FENG SHUI

Macau

The **Human**

Between

Heaven
(Kun Yam Godess)

&

Earth
(The ancient Chinese Coin for earthly abundance)

MACAU
The Author in Chinese New Year of the Snake,
between Heaven & Earth

Using the symbolic Ba Gua
for marketing purposes with
T-Shirts

Fig 17

4

How to do Feng Shui your environment

Every human habitat, is embedded in a context, and the balance for that environment should take your personal situation and needs in considerations. Feng Shui deals with those contexts so you need to start with an analysis of individual needs and intentions.

Intention is the basic ingredient of any solution, and it should be established before any Feng Shui intervention. You can use the tools from Part II Feng Shui your life, as a basis for this evaluation and definition.

A summary on how to approach the Space acupuncture of Feng Shui, is described below, as a guide and reference on how to start the analysis of your location and property, and to apply the different solutions explained earlier in this part of the book.

1- Feng Shui the External environment

Start by looking around your building and locate the surroundings with highest and lowest points, check the general configurations and sources of negative energy, together with potential geopathological sources. Refer to the arm chair configuration explained above and sharp angles or roads, pointing at you.

Now access your building and check the entrance door, its direction and front view, is it large and open to invite light energy to enter?

Do you have a nice view when you get out in the morning? Or is it closed and dark? Are there any trees or other buildings blocking the alley or the access? What is the main entrance location in the Ba Gua?

2- Interior design Feng Shui

Get into the property and feel the main quality and quantity of energy. You may refer to the questionnaire below to access it easier:

- Is the energy blocked or does it flows easily?
- Is it more Yin or more Yang?
- What is the predominant element represented in the room?
- Or is there to many furniture to block the flow?
- Is there a slow moving energy, or you have a long alley where the Chi flows to fast to allow harmony and stability?
- Is it dark or sunny?
- Are there many angles, dead corners or sharp points?
- Is there any beam on the ceiling breaking or separating spaces?
- Over the beds?
- What are the rooms in the front part of the house?
- What are the rooms in the back part?
- What is the first thing that captures your attention when you enter the room?
- What is the general feeling you have?
- Where are the darker and shadow areas?
- What is the dominant smell?

After this general evaluation of the whole property, get into each room and ask yourself the same issues, checking them with the purpose you designed the area for.

3- Space acupuncture with Ba Gua

Finally draw a Map of the location and setup the Ba Gua Matrix drawing a square or a rectangle over it and dividing each wall in three parts to map each of the 9 Lo Shu areas. Do this for,

- The whole Map or drawing of the house
- Each and every room

Pay special attention to main door and stairways, kitchen, bed rooms, office, dining room, living room, toilets.

Make a specific **list** for the whole house and each of its departments, with:

Intent and objective
Unbalances
Solutions
Expected result
Timing

Now start from Lo Shu area numbers 3 – 4 – 5 – 6 – 7 – 8 – 9 – 1 - 2 (see the Flying stars path on part III further on), and implement the specific Feng Shui solutions for every detected need.

5

Action Plan Check List

After analyzing the house location and its main areas and matching them with your life strengths and weaknesses, you should design a detailed action plan for the each case as the one for Lucy explained fully in the annex of the book.

"Check List"

The Feng Shui for your Home and Work environment, should focus on solutions to help you to achieve the objectives defined for a full life balance or to achieve some specific goals.

At the same time you will balance the five elements and the Yan/Yang of your basic nature. This evaluation is based on your Personal Feng Shui (part III), that represent your heaven's luck or determinism in your life.

For Lucy's case study in the annex, this means mostly reduce the excessive water associated with emotions, and promote wood and fire, related to activity and external image, together with reinforcement of a strong center with element earth, to consolidate and give a solid basis to all possible developments.

Furthermore, you should correct any hindrances associated with the actual location of home and work, with the necessary Feng

Shui cures. So the following processes would be recommended to analyze your home and work location and environment.

ENVIRONMENTAL AND LOCATION SOLUTIONS

<u>The External Environment</u>

History of the location
Geo-pathology
General location and surrounding landscape
Entrance door

<u>The Internal Environment</u>

Ba Gua Location of main house areas Strengths and Weaknesses
Kitchen
Bed room
Living room
Toilets
Office

<u>General FENG SHUI Solutions</u>

Energy quality and quantity
5 Elements cures
Yin Yang cures
Ba Gua cures for specific rooms and mansions

<u>Other energetic cures</u>

Lights
Mirrors
Plants
Symbols
Others

<u>*Main room of the house, and* specific solutions</u> to implement:

Solution 1:

    Type of solution and tools
    Intention
    Affirmation

Solution 2:

    Type of solution and tools
    Intention
    Affirmation

Solution ....:

Solution 3:

    Type of solution and tools
    Intention
    Affirmation

Solution ....:

Solution 4:

    Type of solution and tools
    Intention
    Affirmation

Solution ....:

Solution 5:

    Type of solution and tools
    Intention
    Affirmation

Solution ....:

PART II

Feng Shui your Life

PART II

Feng Shui your Life

"Yes, there is a Nirvana;
It is leading your sheep
to a green pasture,
and putting your child
to sleep, and in writing the
last line of your poem"
Kahlil Gibbran

This is the starting point for the whole process, when you make the initial evaluation of what is exceeding, missing or just not pleasing you in your life actually.

We will use for this purpose the Feng Shui Wheel of Life validated through time and introduced to you in the first part of the book as the Magic Square or Ba Gua, together with the main Coaching tools and concepts allowing you to analyze and act over each area of your life..

This is a conscious evaluation about where the choices you made brought you so far, and how much you like them or not.

After finishing this assessment, I suggest you to go through the Personal Feng Shui in part III, where you will find the evaluation of your destiny, life path and human relations compatibility, together with your time line, all of which will help you to highlight and make sense of your more or less conscious situation.

From there, you proceed to integrate it all in one effective Life Coach process, in part IV, after what you may design the detailed Specific Plan on Coaching for Abundance.

A complete case study in the Annex, will illustrate how you can use and integrate all this information in a clear and simple Master Plan.

1

The Feng Shui "Wheel of Life", and the Matrix of the 9 Mansions

For this analysis we will apply the same Lo Shu Matrix, used to analyze the energy of rooms, buildings, and properties, but now focusing on how this structure works in the upper level of your Life specific dimensions.

The LO SHU with the 9 Mansions, the matrix of the nine areas, is based on the Later Heaven *Ba Gua* explained in the previous chapters which is the main tool used for interventions on your environment. These will shape your wheel of life.

The different areas of the Lo Shu are sequentially organized according to the energetic path known as the "Flying Stars", a specific sequence of analysis, aiming to strengthen the power of each intervention. The secret drawing of this path is similar to the shape of the old symbol of the Atlantis Seal.

For greater efficiency, it is recommended that you follow that order, as we do all along the next chapters where you will find exercises that help you recreate the energy of happiness, peace, development, harmony, freedom and abundance.

Start now!

2

Life Mansions, polarities and interdependence

Interpreting the Feng Shui Life Mansions based on the Lo Shu magic square, allow us to perceive how each area of your life or "Mansion", is opposed to another one creating an axis of interdependence and polarity between each pair, offering a global view of their interaction, as we show you in the next paragraphs.

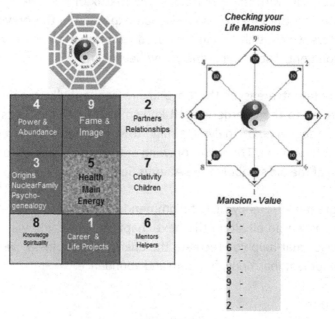

Fig 18
Evaluate your Life Mansions

Mansion 3, your "Roots, Nuclear Family and Psycho-Genealogy" opposing and therefore closely related to *Mansion 7 "Creativity and Children"*, illustrating how where you come from and your social references inner drives and comfort zones, may opposed to your path or directions in the life you create, based on your personal creativity and through raising children, as the next step in the evolution of your personal and psycho-genealogical line.

Mansion 4 "Power and Abundance", in contrast to Mansion 6 "Friends and Protectors", highlights the relationship between your achievements, full life and abundance, to the support of friends, helpers you rely on and surround you, as well as your own capacity of helping other people.

Mansion 5 "Health and Base-Energy" is the central area of the Pa Kua, and related to the main Chi or vital energy of your life, together with your body and your psycho somatic health.

Mansion 8 "Knowledge and spirituality", is opposed to *Mansion 2 "Relationships, and partnerships"*, showing the existing connection between the ability to create and maintain stable relationships with wisdom and spiritual alignment that allows you to leave the co-dependencies and establish healthy links within synergetic autonomy based on love and compassion, which is understanding and mutual acceptance.

Mansion 9 "Image Projection, Projects and Self-knowledge" is polarized by *Mansion 1"Career and Life Prospects"*, showing the interaction known as "Law of Attraction". It means that you attract what you believe and stand for in your life, as well as your shadow issues, which in turn create what you are, a permanent auto-adjusting balance within your projects, as the Yin Yang forces of fire and water.

Finally, in the matrix of the 9 Mansions Ba Gua. We can see further connections, namely the relation between mansions of abundance in life in mansion 4, related with your knowledge and spiritual alignment in mansion 8, together with yourself and projected image in mansion 9, creating the production cycle: wood – fire - earth.

Also the connection between mansions 1, 2 and 8, referring to how your partners (2) together with your helpers and mentors (6), support your life projects (9).

The Flying Stars 9 years cycle, in part III, will illustrate further all these processes along the individual time line.

We propose you now to identify and interpret the other connections and interrelations within the meaning of the mansions with the following numbers. These will create the neurological connections to allow you a more integrated approach to your life settings.

Try the following triangles:

A: 3 – 2 - 6
B: 2 – 3 - 9
C: 4 - 7 – 8

Did you acquired any insights?

A:

B:

C:

3

Inside your Life

For a start, let's identify your current situation, in each one of the 9 areas of the Feng Shui Matrix for your life mansions, to have a first general perspective on the actual life balance.

Using Fig 18 from the previous chapter, fill in the "values" field for each mansion using 0 totally unsatisfactory, to 10 for totally satisfactory, and mark these values on the respective axis over the *Wheel of Life* graphic.

The particular analysis of each Mansion, will start by Mansion3 since it is the area of our roots are, and where our genealogy is represented: the beginning. Then, following the order of Flying Stars, the secret path within the Lo Shu Magic Square, of cyclic impermanence, we proceed towards the directions of arrows, as show, in the image.

The shape of ancient Atlantis seal

Flying Stars Secret Path

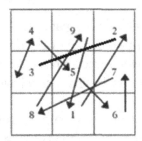

Mansion 3 · Psycho-Genealogy and institutional references

Zhèn (Thunder)

This trigram figures the Thunder and is associated with the element Wood and the eldest son; it represents the East direction (E).

The Mansion of our Psycho-Genealogy, values, inherited beliefs and behaviors, archetypes and institutional references, the house of our ancestors, guides and all the important landmarks of our lives and our sacred contract as the basis of our mission and vision of life.

The Genosociogram (family tree drawn from memory) is the most important tool for understand and manage family issues. It is the genealogical path made from memories, where you write the most important events of family life with details, which are used to provide an overview on the full familiar scenario. This exercise very often causes a very liberating emotional shock!

Our behavior originates, for some psychologists, from our memories which are organized in a quite specific way. These behaviors have little to do with your current life, and their roots are usually found in the past, where your beliefs - either limiting or liberating ones -, are created.

One of the most limiting believes is when you consider that you cannot be better than your parents, so you start a reduction process in your family development, passing this belief to your own children and so on. These positive or negative beliefs are analyzed in the area of Gua 7.

Living according to our values or employ these values to achieve our life goals is the third main part of the trilogy: vision/mission/values, and it is linked to memories, beliefs, archetypes, and other elements that shaped our reticular formation, where the main filters of the mind are located. These values are the ones that determine the perception of reality, our personal mythology and the search of our soul.

Let's check now your roots and purpose in life with a practical exercise. Take some time and a Deeep Breath....

EXERCISE: *My life*

My Mission in life, or my "personal legend" is...

_____

_____

_____

My Vision of Life is...

_____

_____

_____

Who were my childhood heroes, and who where those I wished to look like, at the time?
What are their characteristics?

_____

_____

_____

This call for awareness from "how we do things the way we do" allows us to optimize the apparent paradox in our relations to older people, between learning and showing respect from their irreplaceable life experience, and our decision or ability to drop and change old habits unconsciously repeated.

Not only some of these customs have lost their meaning, but most of them will also have become harmful to you: think of some diet habits or limiting decisions that have hurt you throughout your life, for example, or think of those who decided to believe, unconsciously, that they can never do something their soul demands to fulfill their dreams.

Values and activities

The values are basically filters of evaluation. They are parameters that rule our unconscious way to decide whether our actions are good or bad, right or wrong. Values are organized hierarchically, and they are also responsible for how we feel about the actions we take.

We all have different values and resulting internal models of the world. In the communication with yourself or interaction with others, whenever your model of the world is not in compliance with your values or the values of the other, conflict arises. Common values are the fuel for long term relations.

Values are what bring us closer or set us far apart, they are our attractions or repulsion in life. Basically, they are a deep unconscious system of beliefs of what is important, what is positive or negative to us.

The range of values may vary depending on the context in which we operate, in other words, possibly the values we have in a loving relationship are different than those we show in our professional life, and if they are not, it probably means we will have problems in both areas.

Let's see how we can evaluate the life you have created, through your values.

EXERCISE: *Values and Activities*

In your life, what is most important to you?

First make a list of 8 to 15 (at least five) elements, without thinking about their relative importance.

This exercise will illustrate your Personal Values and their relation to your main Activities.

1. What is more important for you in your life (your five top values):

    1- _____
    _____
    2- _____
    _____
    3- _____
    _____
    4- _____
    _____
    5- _____
    _____

2. Select he 5 main activities of your current life:

    A _____
    _____
    B _____
    _____

C _____
   _____

D _____
   _____

E _____
   _____

3. Fill in the next map for each main activity, with the level of every one of the Five Values above fulfilled for each daily Activity.

Values range from 1 to 5 (1 min to 5 max), of how much each activity fulfills every value:

Activities (A, B, C, D, E)

Values	A	B	C	D	E	Total
1						
2						
3						
4						
5						

TOTAL A.=

5. Analysis of results:

Now evaluate the contribution of the main activities to fulfill your values, as well as which of the main values are met by this current structure of activities.

> **A-** Results from Rows tells you how much of each value is achieved by your main actual activities.
>
> *A1-Add the values of each row and write the result in the total column.*
>
> *A2-Now divide each total by 5. That is the average for each value fulfillment*

B- Results from Columns tells you how much of each activity is contributing for the achievement of your main values satisfaction.

B1-Add the values of each column and write the result below the total column.

B2-Now divide each total by 5. That is the average for each activity contribution to your actual wellbeing.

How can you improve it?

Mansion 4 · Abundance and Power

Xùn (Wind)

This trigram pictures the Wind and is associated with the element Wood and the eldest daughter. It represents the direction Southeast (SE).

Abundance, the gradual and steady accumulation of pleasure, assets, power and all sorts of blessings across your life. The very concept of abundance goes far beyond material wealth and has to do with your ability to create and accept happiness, well-being, harmony, inner peace, love, and everything else to reach plenitude.

We all know people called "neurotic's" that live a hard life because of things that never happened in the past (events that only existed in their own perception), living as if they will never die; on the other hand there are also normal people that suffers because of things that never will happen in the future, (like expecting that the future will bring something or some situation that guarantees them a better, more abundant or happier life), so they will die as if they had never lived.

Your present situation was generated by your thoughts and what you did in the past, as well as your future will depend on what you think and do today.. Ask yourself,

- How many times are you focusing yourself mainly on problems from your past?

- How many times you dont even know anymore what you want?
- Where are you putting your mental energy – in your fears or your ambitions?
- Do I feel worthy of this abundance?
- How much pleasure can I stand?
- Is this the life I want?
- Have you ever thought that the current facts exist only because they depend on your actual attitude?
- What if you were to change the way you act conditioned by the past and replace it with an attitude most useful for you now?

The quality of your life will depend on the quality of your questions about it.

Change your Attitude *Now*, and you will already have changed the past (the experiences that created that attitude), and by the same way you are preparing a new future!

Take the power to co-create your life through learning from the past, freeing yourself of its weight, and planning the future in full creative freedom, which depends exclusively on what you do at the present moment.

Remember to place the energy on what you want, not on what you don't want. State your goals in positive.

EXERCISE: *I deserve abundance*

Attitude:
Do I have an attitude focused on abundance or do I live based on control and limitations?

Merit:
Do I believe I deserve and accept all that the universe has to offer me? Do I feel that I deserve recognition and all I want or am I involved in the plot of "perverse perfectionism"?

_____

Fears and limitations:

Which of my current limitations are self-imposed?

What fears are conditioning my intentions, therefore attracting what I most fear?

Cultivating a correct attitude and freeing yourself of the limitations, fears and low self-esteem, the syndrome of "not worthy", you can concentrate in the behavioral flexibility essential to make the most useful decisions in each given time and thus travel the road of excellence.

Can you recognize your difficulties and manage to turn them into triumphs?

There are no failures only answers to everything we do. If what you are doing don't work, do something else! Successful people see their problems as learning opportunities and a way to improve.

- What have you learned from your last problem?
- Do you believe being capable to assume your responsibilities?
- Do you rely on the opinion of others to evaluate your own work?
- Do you take time to assess and recognize the results and value of your own work?

If you live to satisfy the expectations of others you will never satisfy your own!

The relationship with people around you, friends, mentors, protectors, and their influence on the way you reach this state of abundance, involves the ability to give and receive and becomes evident whithin the polarization with Area 6 of the Ba Gua.

Other dimension have to do with your personal will power, the inner power to live the present moment fully. Remember the Time and the Moment you may change ... is NOW!!!

Let's remind ourselves of a famous metaphor...

A tourist went to India in order to visit a famous sage.
The tourist was surprised to see that the wise man lived in a small room very simple and full of books.
The only pieces of furniture were a bed, a table and a bench.
- Where is your furniture? - Asked the tourist.
And the wise man, and quickly looked around and asked also:
- And where is yours ...?
- Mine? – answered the tourist surprised. - But I'm here on a trip!
- Me too... - concluded the wise man.

The *"Road of the Useful Attitude"*, a simple recipe to create a life of Quality, through an internal change, is based on the following precepts:

- Have the **COURAGE** to change everything you can change. Do not live below your capabilities.
- Have the **PATIENCE** to accept everything you cannot change. Do not waste energy which is needed for other things.
- Have the **INTELLIGENCE** to distinguish one from the other. Live at the top.

Mansion 5 · Central Palace, Health and Energy

T'ai Chi

This central mansion represents number 5 and the Yellow Earth element, strong and centered, in the Magic Square Ba Gua.

This Palace corresponds to the vital energy of the person and it represents your health, beyond the mere physical perspective. It includes the quality of life and the general well-being related with the sense of fulfillment based on your consistence and alignment with your mission and vision of life together with the harmonious relationships with family and friends, the respect for your ancestors, the recognition of your personality and the physical development allowing you to enjoy health well-being at all levels.

Your personal space

Some questions regarding your personal space may highlight who and where you are easily, because existing in a 3Dimensional space world implies that I have time and space for myself without what I hardly exist. This is mainly why to have a personal intimate safe and inviolable space (external and internal), is central to our balance. Time and Space, define our existence, so without any of these two elements, our life is called into question.

How much time do you have for yourself, to be centered, to be connected, for eating, for your hygiene, physical care? Ultimately, anything you do and achieve to maintain your interior connection and your psycho-physical development.

Questions:

Do I have room for myself?
Where is my "sacred space" in the house?
Is there/isn't there one? ~
Where is it located?
Is this the place *I* want?

Your frontiers, your own limits and respect for others, partners, family, friends, associations, etc., are essential to quality of life. The balance of these limits and the creation of an inner space of security, must, therefore, be one of our priorities and basic responsibilities.

YOUR *PERSONAL CHI* OR VITAL ENERGY

You can activate this energy through techniques such as: *Yoga*, to stabilize your body and your mind; through *Chi Kung*, to cultivate the energy; through *Tai Chi*, to set the energy in motion and; through *Reiki*, to provide more vital energy into your physical, emotional, mental and spiritual body, and also stretching with Pilates, and other Body Work techniques.

Look in your area where you can go and sign up for these courses. Practice at least three times a week.

Your health and its signals

Huang Di 黄帝, known in the West as the Yellow Emperor, probably ruled China from 2698 BC until 2599 BC. He is considered the ancestor of all Chinese of the Han dynasty and the creator of the ancient Chinese calendar.

During his ruling, Huang Di became especially interested in health and human condition and he curiously inquired information from physicians about the medical traditions at the time.

From the records of conversations between Huang Di and his physicians came the work now known as NeiJing - "The Yellow Emperor's Inner Classic". This work is considered one of the key books of the traditional Chinese medicine and is divided in two books of 81 chapters each.

We summarize, in this chapter, some basic principles on health and quality of life, in the light of this ancient knowledge, and its connections with the body acupuncture of Feng Shui.

This 5th Mansion, deals with the vital energy of the individual, together with health issues. In anatomical terms of the Body Ba Gua, corresponds to the six viscera (Fu) and the three organs located below the diaphragm.

The body Ba Gua is the main energy map to access and rebalance your body electric linking all psycho-physiological balance, through our "Quantum Energy Network".

The connection between our human, earthly and heaven energies is processed through special points, in the physical body.

the Acupuncture meridians,
the chakras network associated with our hormones,
the nervous system, namely the autonomic nervous system.

These are the main energy circuits in the human body where the energy flows allowing us to interact with the body electric for analysis and balancing of our human psycho-bio-energetic bodies, throughout the four levels of healing: physical, mental, emotional and spiritual.

The Yellow Emperor and the Energy Channels in Human Body

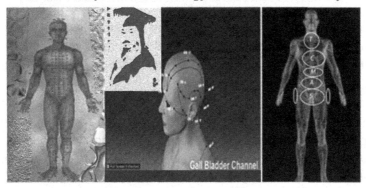

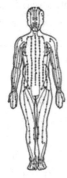

**Acupuncture
Meridians
and the
Chackra Vortex
Network**

Fig 19

This Physical / Etheric interface, are the points at the body surface that interconnect and impacts the full individual and is based on three main maps, that we will briefly describe below:

the Nervous System,
the Chackras Vortex
the Acupuncture Meridians

The Nervous System,

Receiving outside stimuli, the nervous system allow us to react and adapt to external conditions, and it interacts with ourselves acting upon the muscles and the hormones, which are the ultimate controller of our behaviors.

These behaviors can be more or less automatic according to the location where the reaction is based on; for example, if you touch a very hot surface, you will redraw your hand very fast, with an automatic primal response, coming from your peripheral nerves, which is very different from a more reasoned reaction and decision to run away, if you see a wild animal coming to you, which is based more on the logical thinking of our cerebral cortex, that was the last part of the brain developed in humans.

The autonomic part of our nervous system, is the one responsible to keep our survival mechanisms running even while you are sleeping.

The two branches of this main commander of our physiology, are the Parasympathetic managing the relaxation process and activating all our vegetative systems like breathing and digesting, and the Sympathetic which activates the stress response throwing all energy to the fight or fly response, through the adrenaline and cortisol cascade.

the Chackra Network

The main Chackras are 7 even if some schools define other more etheric and spiritual ones, below and above the body. They are energy vortex that cross the body in specific locations and their spinning speed is connected to what is called their degree of "openness" or closed.

They have specific connections to each group of hormones, emotions, organs, mental patterns, and all the human dimensions.

The Chackra network is also the framework of what is commonly called "intuitive medicine" and the basis of the Ayurveda / Indian approach to energetic healing.

From Top down, the 7 most common chackras are,

Chackra 7 – Crown, connected to
* Pineal gland – spiritual connection and harmony of the whole system

Chackra 6 – Third Eye, connected to
* Pituitary gland – Intuition

Chackra 5 – Throath, connected to
* Thyroide gland – Speech and Expression of inner truth

Chackra 4 – Heart, connected to
* Thymus gland – Love and compassion

Chackra 3 – Plexus, connected to
* Stomach - Self worth and will power

Chackra 2 – Navel, connected to
* Adrenals and pancreas – creativity and sexual relationships

Chackra 1 – Base chackra, connected to
* Sex organs – material security

The Acupuncture Meridians

In the Chinese Traditional Medicine, there are three ways to access and manage energy in the human body: the Acupuncture meridians, Meditation, Oriental Herbs. As the main energy channels, the Acupuncture meridians, are the most quick and effective way of analysis and rebalancing.

The main meridians used in Chinese medicine are 14 and they are mapped since more then 5.000 years ago, being so far the more resilient and tested healing system on earth resisting centuries of proofing, although only recently, in the last 30 to 40 years it has been fully integrated in western integrative medicine and healers practice and knowledge.

There are 14 Acupressure Meridians which have somatic and emotional connections:

Meridian Conception (CV)

When balanced promote de emotions of Success and self-respect

When this meridian is blocked, is associated with the emotions of shame, failure and overwhelmed

Meridian Governor (GV)

When balanced promote de emotions of Supporting and trusted

When this meridian is blocked, is associated with the emotions of Distrustful, competitive and unsupported

Meridian Small Intestine (SI)

When balanced promote de emotions of Joy, equality and appreciation.

When this meridian is blocked, is associated with the emotions of sorrow, inferiority, unappreciated

Meridian Triple Warmer (TW)

When balanced promote de emotions of hope, lightness and harmony.

When this meridian is blocked, is associated with the emotions of Hopelessness, heaviness and loss of faith

Meridian Heart (H)

When balanced promote de emotions of love, forgiveness, self-appreciation

When this meridian is blocked, is associated with the emotions of anger, hate, insecure and jealous.

Meridian Circulation and Sex (CS)

When balanced promote de emotions of relaxation, intimacy, satisfaction.

When this meridian is blocked, is associated with the emotions of blame, stubbornness, and regrets.

Meridian Spleen (Sp)

When balanced promote de emotions of confidence and faith in the future.

When this meridian is blocked, is associated with the emotions of regrets, anxiety and mental rigidity

Meridian Stomach (St)

When balanced promote de emotions of empathy, tranquil and contentment

When this meridian is blocked, is associated with the emotions of worry, judgmental

Meridian Lung (L)

When balanced promote de emotions of enthusiasm, humble and tolerant.

When this meridian is blocked, is associated with the emotions of sadness, intolerance and depression.

Meridian Large Intestine (LI)

When balanced promote de emotions of self-worth and letting go.

When this meridian is blocked, is associated with the emotions of unworthy, attach to old stuff and inner flexibility.

Meridian Bladder (B)

When balanced promote de emotions of peace and harmony, self-control.

When this meridian is blocked, is associated with the emotions of trauma and frustration, impatience, restless.

Meridian Kidney (K)

When balanced promote de emotions of inner peace, self-confidence, sexual strength, security

When this meridian is blocked, is associated with the emotions of fear, insecurity, anxiety, procrastination and grief

Meridian Gall Bladder (GB)

When balanced promote de emotions of compassion, loved.

When this meridian is blocked, is associated with the emotions of abandonment, resentment, holding non expressed anger

Meridian Liver (Lv)

When balanced promote de emotions of happiness, contentment, free to change, knowledge and spiritual conexion.

When this meridian is blocked, is associated with the emotions of, anger, defensive, unhappiness and being stuck.

Biological Clock

These meridians have been traditionally associated with specific hours of activation and each of the 12 earthly branches of the Pillars of Destiny, as we will see in the next part of the book, as follows,

HOUR	BRANCH	ORGAN / MERIDIAN
2300-0100	Rat	Gall Bladder
0100-0300	Ox	Liver
0300-0500	Tiger	Lungs
0500-0700	Rabbit	Large Intestine
0700-0900	Dragon	Stomach
0900-1100	Snake	Spleen
1100-1300	Horse	Heart
1300-1500	Goat	Small Intestine
1500-1700	Monkey	Bladder
1700-1900	Rooster	Kidney
1900-2100	Dog	Master of the Heart
2100-2300	Pig	Triple Warmer

The Technological up-grade: electro-physiology devices

Together with this twelve plus two traditional meridians, a German doctor R. VOLL, in the middle of last century developed with western electrical technology what is called the "electro acupuncture" that have found some more subtle channels that are called the VOLL meridians. This process uses electric stimulation to access the energy meridians instead of the classic needles that some people fear.

Some up to date machines are today present in the market and allow practitioners to measure and balance all the energy channels. They are named as Biofeedback or Neuro Bio-feedback, like the SCIO, or Bio-ressonance, like the Biolaser, (see also www. neuroquantum.net).

With the huge technology development from last decade the possibility to evaluate and transfer in real time trends and volumetric data from biological sensors, an enormous amount of sensors for capturing electrical signals from the body appeared, together with specific software for analysis and feedback, giving birth to what is called the Electrophysiology branch of medicine, monitoring more than 100 data channels simultaneously like EEG, ECG, EMG, PPT, Motility, Respiration, HRV, GSR, btween many others.

Also more recently appeared in the west, some techniques that allow incredible results relieving physical and emotional pain and fears, and reprograming distorted reactions, with digipuncture based approaches, also known Tapping, namely the TFT – Though Field Therapy-, and the EFT –emotional freedom technique (see my book on EFT for Emotional freedom, by EDAF publishers).

Besides connections to the human organs and hormones, these energy networks are also connected to the emotional profiles and to mental patterns.

The Quantum Network of energy fields needs to support its operation, the neurological network of 100 billion neurons and their synaptic connections that manage all our automatic, semi-automatic, and reasoned responses to environment stimuli, through acting on our hormonal levels and muscular tonus.

FUNCTIONS of Autonomical Nervous System

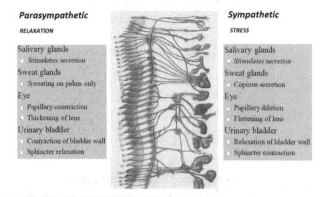

Parasympathetic	Sympathetic
RELAXATION	STRESS
Salivary glands	Salivary glands
Stimulates secretion	*Stimulates secretion*
Sweat glands	Sweat glands
Sweating on palms only	Copious secretion
Eye	Eye
Papillary constriction	Papillary dilation
Thickening of lens	Flattening of lens
Urinary bladder	Urinary bladder
Contraction of bladder wall	Relaxation of bladder wall
Sphincter relaxation	Sphincter contraction

Technological Devices to access the electrical body: Biofeedback, Bioresonance, EEG ,ECG ,...

Fig 20

Most of our patterns are programed in the reaction of the autonomic nervous system that connect our stress response – the sympathetic subsystem -, to the neuro vegetative parasympathetic network, and is connected with all spinal nerves, to our organic and emotional being.

The map of the body and the concepts of Yin / Yang

The concepts of Yin / Yang are relative and not absolute. The "physical" heart is a Yin organ, but it has a contracting effect, pushing blood through channels (veins) which is Yang.

Lo Shu representation of the
human body and its symbolism
Water (1) - Wood (3,4) - Fire - (9) - Earth (2,5,8) - Metal (6,7)

4	9	2
Left foot	Heart - Chest - throat Head - Face	Right foot
3	5	7
Thorax left side	Viscera and Abdominal organs	Thorax Right side
8	1	6
Left hand	Members Hips Genitals	Right hand

Using Yin Yang concepts for Diagnosys

YIN	YANG
INTERNAL	EXTERNAL
COLD	HOT
DEFICIENCY	EXCESS
CHRONIC	ACUTE

Functions of the Yin / Yang	
YIN	YANG
COOL	HEAT
FEED	TRANSFORM
HUMIDIFY	PROTECT
RELAX	KEEP

Physiological Links Yin	Physiological Links Yang
Blood	Circulation
Lymph	Secretion
Mucous	Discharge
Urine	Peristalsis
Sweat	Perspiration
Nutrition	Respiration

Fig 21

YIN ORGANS - the internal organs of anabolism are "physical" with built-in storage and assimilation:

Liver, heart, spleen, lungs and kidneys.

YANG ORGANS – the external organs of catabolism are "empty", with elimination functions:

Gallbladder Intestine, Small Intestine, Stomach and Bladder.

For diagnostic purposes the concepts of Yin / Yang in traditional Chinese medicine are administered as shown in fig 21.

The *Yin* organs inside our bodies are more protected from external influences in relation to the most exposed *Yang* organs such as skin and muscles.

The lowest part of the body (feet, legs, hips), are in contact, and closer to the ground, and therefore it is more *Yin* that the upper body, able to move freely, most *Yang*, your back for instance, is more *Yang* and the front of your body is more *Yin*.

Finally, the three energies, Heaven, Earth, and Human, are also presented in the Human body.

Heavenly Chi, the energetic center located in the middle of the eyebrows but inside the head,

Earth Chi is located roughly three inches below the navel, and the

Human Chi three inches below the middle high of the individual.

These locations correspond roughly to the Chackras 2, 3 and 6, or the Third Eye, in the Ayurveda tradition from India.

The Face Ba Gua, for health and wellness

To evaluate a person face, you can just superimpose the Ba Gua Matrix over it when you look face to face, so the area for Children would be on your right side and on its left side, the family area will be on your left side and its right side. Fame will be in the middle of the forehead and career on the chin.

Next you can analyze every specific spot or signal you may find in each area of the Face Ba Gua, its shape and color, to understand what may be involved, there.

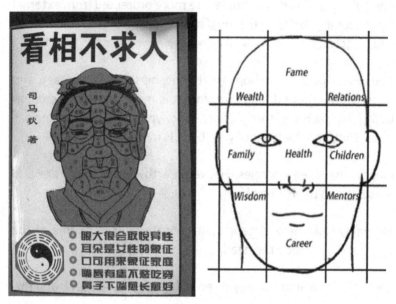

Fig 22

Regarding this reading in the Wealth area, for instance, the Green, Pink and Purple colors are the wealthiest ones and the White is the worst. Reds meaning your fortune is already settled.

The Mind-Body Connections
Mini Psychosomatic Guide

It is widely accepted today that the body and the mind act in a completely integrated and (w)holistic way, where body, mind and spirit interact on an ongoing basis to maintain balance or in other words, the homeostasis of life. The study of the relationship between body and mind, as well as the warning signals sent by both, is the domain of Psychosomatic studies.

This whole book is dedicated to encouraging the importance of listening, understanding and reacting to the different external and internal signals to find the path of harmony and excellence of life.

We already understood the importance of listening to the body signals and take in consideration our mental and behavioral patterns.

Now we suggest you to perform an exercise based on the next short psychosomatic guide from most studied and consensual accepted relationships.

EXERCISE

After checking your main complaints in the list below, and evaluate their psychological and mental patterns, write the affirmation statements corresponding to each psychosomatic problem affecting you, or those around you.

Use as reference, the affirmations on the Mini Guide that follows, about examples over the most common health problems, and according to the rules of the last chapter *"The Magic Sentence!"*.

Check and confirm the dates when the problem begun, and analyze them together with the facts that preceded 1 to 3 months before the appearance of the symptoms, in order to make sense and find the root cause of every issue. Those may have caused the mental patterns referred.

MENTAL CAUSATION of Common Diseases

We present you below the mental causations of the most common diseases, together with the affirmation patterns you may use to liberate and heal the issue. For each disease you will find:

1. **ISSUE or Disease**
2. **PSYCHOSOMATIC BASIS, or the mental disrupted patterns affecting the body balance**
3. **AFIRMATIONS and NEW THOUGHT PATTERNS to return to Health and Wellness**

Abscess
Hurts, affronts, revenge.
I do not allow my thoughts to irritate me. I am at peace.

Acne
Not accepting the self-Dislike of the self.
I love & accept myself where I am right now. I am wonderful

Accidents
Rebellion against authority. Belief in violence. Anger
Peace & security. I love & accept all my life

Adenoids
Family friction, arguments. Child feeling unwelcome.
This child is wanted & welcome.

Addictions
Self-rejection, fear, lack of love.
I am only addicted to love myself. Nothing has power over me.

Aging
Social beliefs, old thinking.
I love & accept myself at every age.Each age is perfect

Alcoholism
Feeling of futility, inadequacy.
Release the past. I am worthwhile. I love & accept myself now.

Allergies
Who are you allergic to?
I am at peace. The world is safe & friendly.

Anemia
Lack of joy, no interest in life. The "Yes! but," attitude
My world is filled with joy. I am interested in everything.

Appendicitis
Fear. Fear of life. Blocking the flow.
Joy, I relax & let life flow.

Arteriosclerosis
Resistance, tension, narrow mindedness
I am completely open to life & to joy, Life is beautiful.

Arthritis
Bitterness, resentment, criticism, Feeling unloved.
Love, forgiveness. I let others be themselves & I am free.

Asthma
Over-sensitivity, smoother love. Suppressed crying. Feeling muted.
I am free. I take charge of my own life.

Back Problems
Lack of support.
> UPPER; Lack of emotional support,.
>> Holding back love.
> LOWER; lack of financial support.
>> Fear of money.

Life itself supports me. I trust the universe. I freely give love and trust.

: 2

Bedwetting
Fear of parent, usually father.
Love, understanding, compassion

Birth Defects
Karmic. You selected to come that way. We choose our parents. No guilt. You both had something to work out.

Blood Problems
Lack of joy. Lack of circulation of ideas. Stagnant thinking
Joy. Joyous new ideas circulating freely.

Blood Pressure
HIGH; Long standing emotional problem not solved.
LOW; Defeatism, depression, sorrow.
HIGH; I joyously release the past.
LOW I live in the ever joyous now. Life is a joy.

Boils
Anger, boiling over.
I release all anger & resentment.

Bone Problems
Rebelling against authority Bones.
I am at peace with authority. In my world. I am my own authority

Brain Tumor
Incorrect computerized beliefs. Stubborn, refusing to change old patterns.
All of life is change. My growth patterns are ever new.

Breast, Cysts,
Over mothering, over protection.
I am free, & I allow everyone to be free.

Soreness.
Overbearing attitudes.

Bronchitis
Inflamed family environment.
Peace. No one can irritate me.

Burns
Anger. Burning up.
People have no power over me. I am the peace in my enviroment.

Bursitis
Repressed anger, wanting to hit. someone
I release anger in harmless ways. Love releases & relaxes.

Bruises
The little bumps in life.
There is no reason to beat myself up. I am the action of love.

Cancer
Deep secret or grief eating away at the self. Long standing resentment.
There are no secrets. I release all of the past. My present is filled with joy.

Car Sickness
Fear. Bondage. Feeling of being trapped.
I move with ease through time & space, there is no fear.

Cataracts
Dark future. Inability to see ahead.
I am free. Life is eternal & filled with joy.

Cholesterol
Clogging of the channels of joy. Fear of accepting joy.
Joy is normal. My channels of joy are wide open. I love life.

Colds
Confusion, disorder, small hurts.
I am a free thinker. I am at peace in my own mind.

Colitis
Over-exacting parents. I am free. Oppression, defeat. Needs affection
I provide my own joy. Life is eternal.

Constipation
Refusing to release old ideas.   Stinginess.
I release the past. I generously allow life to flow through me.

Coughs
Nervousness, annoyance, criticism. Choking on life
I express myself in a peaceful way. I speak with love.

Cramps
Tension. Gripping, holding on.
I relax & allow life to flow.

Cysts
False growth. Nursing shocks, hurts.
I dissolve old angers. Nothing can hurt me.

Deafness
What don't you want to hear?   Rejection, stubbomess, isolation.
I listen to God. I hear the joys of life. I am part of life.

Diabetes
Deep sense of sorrow.   No sweetness to life.
I allow life to be FUN. I let the past be just that. I accept joy & fun as the basis of my life.

Diarrhea
Getting rid of ideas too fast. Fear. Rejection of the past.
I accept life past, present & future in Divine right order.

Dowagers Hump, Hunchback
Anger behind you. Resentment built up.
I see the past with joy. No one has ever harmed me

Earache
Anger, don't want to hear.
I listen whit love & joyously hear the good & the pleasant.

Eczema
Over-sensitiveness, hurt individuality.   Hurt personality.
I am secure, no one threatens my individuality.

Edema
What or who won't you let go of?
I willingly release all of the past. I am secure & free.

Epilepsy
Rejection of life. Violence against the self. Sense of persecution
I love myself & all of life. Life is eternal joy.

Eye Problems
Not liking what you see. in your own life Fear of the future. Not
seeing Truth.
I see with loving eyes. I like what I see, I see clearly, I see the Truth.

Face
Represents individuality, recognition.
I recognize my own true worth. My individuality is secure.

Fainting
Fear. Can't cope. Blanking out.
I have the power, strength & knowledge to handle everything in my life.

Fatigue
Resistance, boredom. Lack of love for what one does.
I am enthusiastic about life, & filled with energy.

Fevers
Burning up. Anger.
I am the calm expression of peace & love.

Fingers
Fussing over the details in life. FINGERNAILS is over-analyses of tiny details
I relax knowing the wisdom of life takes care of all details.

Foot Problems
Fear of the future and of stepping forward in life. Understanding.
TOES are minor details of the future
I stand in Truth. I move forward with joy. I have spiritual understanding.

Gas Pains
Gripping undigested ideas. Gulping air
I relax & let life flow through me with ease.

Gall Stones
Bitterness. Hard thoughts you cannot seem to dismiss.
Joyous release of the past. Life is sweet and so am I.

Glandular Problems
Imbalance. Lack of order. Poor distribution
I am in total balance. My system is in order.

Glaucoma
Emotional pressure from Long.
No one can ever hurt me, I see with love & tenderness.

Gout
Impatience, anger. Domination.
I release ego & feelings of superiority. I let others be.

Growths
Nursing hurts. False sense of false
Forgiveness. I love myself & will not harm myself.

Gum Problems
Inability to back up decisions once they are made
I am a decisive person. I follow through.

Hands
The ability to grasp & let go of ideas. Fear of new ideas.
I handle all ideas with love & ease.

Halitosis
Rotten attitudes, vile gossip, foul thinking,.
I speak with gentleness & love. I exhale only the good.

Hay Fever
Emotional congestion. Mass beliefs & fear of the calendar
I deny any beliefs in calendars. I am one with ALL of life.

Headaches
Tension, emotional upsets, hurt feelings, uncertainty, fear.
Peace, love, joy, relaxation. In my world all is well.

Heart Problems
Serious emotional problems, long standing.. Lack of joy, rejection
of of life. Belief in strain & pressure
Joy, Love & Peace. I joyfully accept all of life.

Hemorrhoids
Burden, pressure, tension, fear. Afraid to let go
I release all pressure & burdens. I live in the joyous present.

Hepatitis
Fear, anger, hatred. Lives in the seat of anger & primitive emotions.
I let go of everything I no longer need. My consciousness is now
cleansed & my concepts are free, new & vital.

Hernia
Strain, mental loads. Self-punishment. Anger. Incorrect creative
expression.
My life is gentle & harmonious. I love myself with tenderness.

Hip Problems
Fear of going forward in major decisions
I joyfully move forward supported & sustained by the power of life.

Hives
Small hidden fears. Mountains out of molehills.
I am peaceful with the little things in life.

Holding Fluids
What are you afraid of losing?
I release with joy & willingness.

Hypoglycemia
Imbalance in the system. Lack of joy
The acceptance of joy balances my system.

Impotence
Sexual pressure, tension, guilt. Social beliefs. Spite against a
previous mate.
Power. I allow the full power of my sexual principle to operate with
ease & joy.

Indigestion
Fear, dread, anxiety.
I take in the new & easily assimilate it.

Infections
Irritation, anger, annoyance.
Nothing has the power to irritate me. I am peaceful & harmonious.

Influenza
Response to mass negativity & beliefs. Belief in statistics. Fear.
I am not governed by group beliefs or the calendar. I am free from all congestion & influence

Insanity
Escapism, withdrawal. Violent separation from life. Fleeing from family
My mind knows its true identity & I am a creative point of Divine Self Expression.

Insomnia
Tension, guilt, fear.
I release the day and slip into peaceful sleep, knowing that tomorrow will take care of itself.

Itching
Unsatisfied desires, remorse. Punishment for guilt.
Whatever I need will always be here. I accept my good without guilt.

Jaundice
Prejudice. Discolored beliefs.
I feel tolerance & compassion & love for all people.

Kidney Problem
Criticism, sensitivity, disappointment, frustration.
I see only good everywhere. Right action is taking place & I am fulfilled.

Knee Problem
Inflexibility, fear. Ego, pride, inability to bend. Stubborn
Forgiveness, tolerance, compassion. I move forward without
hesitation.

Laryngitis
Fear of voicing opinions, resentment of authority. Anger
I can speak up for myself. I can speak up for myself. I express myself
freely.

Leg Problems
Fear of the future. Legs carry you forward.
I move forward with confidence & joy.

Liver Problem
Depression, repression. Chronic complaints. Liver is the seat of
anger.
I live life through the open space in my heart. I am free to love

Lung Problems
Afraid to take in and give out life.
The breath of life flows easily through me.

Menopause Problems
Fear of no longer being wanted. Self-rejection. Fear of aging.
I am balanced in all changes of cycles & I bless my body with love.

Menstrual Problems
Rejection of one's feminine side. guilt, fear. Belief that the genitals
are sinful or dirty.
I accept myself as beautiful woman with normal feminine processes
& changes. All is well in my body.

Migraine Headaches
Resisting the flow of life. Emotional sprees. Sexual fears
I relax into the flow of life & let life flow through me easily

Mouth Problems
The incapacity to take in ideas. Pre-set opinions, closed mind.
I welcome new ideas & new concepts.

Multiple Sclerosis
Mental hardness, hard-heartedness, iron will, inflexibility.
I no longer try to control. I flow along with the joy of life.

Nails Biting
Spite of a parent. Eating away at the self.
I am **a** mature creative individual. I accept & am secure in my maturity.

Neck
Inflexibility, refusing to see all sides of a question. Stubborn.
I am flexible. I welcome other viewpoints too.

Nerves
Communication. Struggle, rushing,
I am on an endless journey through eternity. Peace, be still.

Nervousness
Fear, anxiety. Confused thinking.
There is nowhere to rush.

Numbness
With holding love or consideration.
I respond to life. I share my feeling & my love. I feel, I feel.

Overweight
Insecurity, self-rejection. Seeking love. Protecting the body. Trying to fulfill the self. Fear of loss Stuffing feelings.
I accept & love myself as I am. I am always secure in spiritual nourishment. I allow myself to feel.

Pain
Congestion, blockage. Belief in bondage. Punishment for guilt.
I release any need for punishment. I let go & let life flow through me.

Paralysis
Fear, escapism, resistance. Shock.
I am one with all of life & I welcome my experiences with joy.

Pneumonia
Desperation, tired of life. Emotional wound. Inner disturbance.
I freely take in Divine Ideas which are filled with the Breath of Life.

Prostate Problem
Giving up, defeatism. Sexual pressure & guilt. Belief in aging.
I accept my manliness. I am eternally powerful. Sex is a pleasure.

Psoriasis
Emotional insecurity. Someone is rubbing you the wrong way.
I am peaceful & secure. I am at ease with all of life.

Rheumatism
Lack of love. Resentment. Chronic bitterness, revenge.
I have compassion for others & for myself. I accept joyful feelings.

Rickets
Emotional malnutrition. Lack of love & security.
I am secure & nourished by the love of the universe.

Sea Sickness
Fear. Fear of death.
There is no death, only change. Life is continuous.

Sciatic
Fear of money & the future. Material fears without reason.
I move into my greater good. My good is everywhere I am secure.

Sinus Problems
Irritation to one person, someone close.
No one has the power to irritate me unless I allow it. Peace, harmony.

Shingles
Prolonged nervous suspense.
I am relaxed in all my thinking & in all my activities. Peace, be still.
I fear not.

Shoulder Problems
Burden bearing, overburdened.
Life is joyous & free, all that I accept is good.

Skin Problems
Threatening the individuality. Lack of security, impatience. RASH:
a babyish way of getting attention.
I accept my individuality. I am emotionally secure. I get attention
in positive ways

Slipped Disc
Indecision. Not feeling emotionally supported by others.
I am courageous & independent. I am supported by life.

Stomach
Not able to assimilate ideas and emotions. Fear of new ideas.
I assimilate new ideas easily. Life agrees with me.

Strokes
Rejection of life. Self-violence. Extreme resistance.
I accept life past, present & future. Life is a joy.

Stuttering
Insecurity. Lack of self-expression.
I am allowed to speak up for myself. I am secure in my own
expression. I communicate with love.

Teeth
Long standing indecisiveness. Incapacity to break down ideas for analysis and decision.
I make my decisions based upon the principles of truth & I feel secure about the outcome of those decisions.

Throat Problem
Blockage in expression. Repressed anger. Emotional hurt swallowed.
I freely express myself with joy. No one can hurt me. I am at peace.

Tonsilitis
Repressed emotions & fear. Gripped anger.
Nothing impedes my good. I allow the free flowing expression of Divine ideas to take place by means of me.

Tuberculosis
Selfishness. Possessiveness. Cruelty. A wasting disease.
I do not choke on life. My thought dwells on great ideas every moment of my life is meaningful.

Tumors
False Growths. Nursed hurts & shocks.
Release, forgiveness. Love dissolves all hurts.

Ulcers
Something eating away at you. Anxiety, fear, tension. Belief in pressure.
Nothing can irritate me. I am peaceful, calm and at easy

Vaginitis
Sexual guilt. Feeling of loss of something or someone loved.
Forms & channels may change, but love is never lost. All parts of my body are beautiful

Varicose Veins
Negativity, resistance. Overworked. Standing in a job you hate. Clogged circulation of ideas. Discouragement.
Feeling I move and live in joy. I love life & I circulate freely.

Veneral
Sexual guilt. Belief that the genitals are sinful or dirty. Need for punishment. & its expression.
I lovingly and joyously accept my sexuality. There is no guilt and no punishment

Warts
Belief in ugliness. Guilt, hate for the self.
I do not advertise ugly thoughts. There is no guilt. I love all of my body.

EXERCISE: *Physical Health Check List*

Evaluate your 6 main *physiological* body systems
(from 0 to 10, the six main systems)

1-Head and brain:
Metaphysical meaning: thinking and mental processes
How is my creativity, and ideas?

2-Respiratory system:
Metaphysical meaning: how I enjoy and flow with life.
How much do you enjoy life?

3-Alimentary system:
Metaphysical meaning: ingestion and absorption
How do I digest things in life, and how I retain life lessons?

J.J. Lupi

4-Urinary system:
Metaphysical meaning: excretion
How do I expel what I do not need anymore?

5-Skeleton:
Metaphysical meaning: Life Structure
How are my support systems in my life? How easy they flow?

6-Genital system:
Metaphysical meaning: Security
How do I secure myself and my family line?

Global energy level:

Sum up the value of each one of the six systems above: _____

Now divide the sum by 6: _____ */ 6 =*

This is the Global Score of your energy evaluation= _____

Mansion 6 · Friends, Protectors and Journeys

乾

Qián (Heaven)

This trigram figures Heaven and is associated with the Metal element, the father, and represents the Northwestern direction (NO).

A good Social Support Network (SSN) is a vital part of our fulfillment as social beings, and lies somewhere between our identity and the integration within the different "tribes" we are connected to, as part of the universal quantum interactions of interdependence.

The therapeutic effect of a good social support allowing you to feel "part" of something greater, is with no doubt, an essential element in recovering the psycho-physical balance, namely in cases of grief, serious losses and bigger traumas.

All your life transitions would be more bearable if you had multiple social identities, for example, if fired from the company where you work and lose your standard peer group, you can maintain and strengthen your self-esteem through your participation in sports, social or volunteer group, and other replacement social groups.

Also in this network of inter-relationships you can find your "models", your human references, people that have already reached what you still aim, like someone with big social success with excellent results in business, creativity, etc.

If they did, we can analyze what they do and how they do it, how they think and how they obtain the results you want now. After this analysis, what remains to be done is to model, or in other words: act as if we were in his/her skin and wait for results.

People like people that are like themselves. According to the law of attraction and empathy, "we draw to ourselves people who are similar to us ", therefore it is important to be aware of what kind of people we attract to our lives and who we are allowing to be part of our universe, just so we are able to change the way we act to attract the life we want to live.

When you want to find interesting and supporting people, answer the following questions, and reflect on them,

Who were the people who helped me in my life?
How did I come to know them?
Where did we meet?
What was I doing when I met them?

Now you know where you can find them!

EXERCISE: *how to deal with people that disturb you*

The following exercise will help you to deal with people who most annoy or disturb your inner peace.

➤ Make a list of all the people that bother you.
➤ For each one of these persons, do the following exercise:

• Create an image of that person as he is looking at you whenever he is disturbing you in anyway. Now, listen to what he usually says in this moment.

- Feel the emotion that his words cause on you and where in your body the disturbance is located,

Now,

➢ Freeze the image.
➢ Make it Black and White.
➢ Push it away and reduce its size to 10%.
➢ Make it spin in the reverse direction of the old emotion,... very fast
➢ Mentally visualize now

- emerging over his skin,
- a red ball over his nose,... large pink ears,... a donkey tail, a BIG mouth
- his voice sound like Donald Duck ... Quack. Quack!
- set up a musical happy background... like a circus music.

Notice now how you feel different!

Take your mind away... think of your next holydays... now,... divert you mind a little and re-think of that person... the emotion is still there ... No?

Isn't it amazing?

Forget versus Forgiveness

Finally, one of the major factors limiting your freedom of action are ongoing conflicts waiting for solutions, as well as pending and holding forgiveness.

These blockages put lots of weight over your shoulders paralyzing your capacity for action. Your freedom and relational harmony is the result of their effective management and resolution.

Forgive and manage your conflicts and misunderstood, remember that you are holding to something or someone, that most of the times does not even remember you, or "the situation" anymore. Forgive and let go!

Your problem will no longer be a problem not when you forget it but when it does not bother you anymore.

Mansion 7 · Creativity and Children

Duì (Lake)

This trigram represents the Lake and is associated with the element Metal, the youngest daughter, and represents the Western direction (W).

Children have always been the ultimate symbol of creativity. Free from the constraints and patterns imprinted throughout life, we see emerging the creativity of young people in the today's world: people like Mark Zuckerberg, creator of Facebook is a good example as well as Steve Jobs or Bill Gates who created Microsoft (in the 70's) when he was still young, which is now the best-known software company in the world.

These energies are represented in house 7 and associated with the West direction.

How you relate with your children set you up your family line, and is with no doubt, one of the key factors of stability, coherence and wellness in life.

Beware of the patterns you transmit, mostly unspoken and unconsciously through your behaviors and attitudes and even your feelings. These imprints start soon in the gestation period and will be stronger before four years old when more than 75% will be already imprinted.

THREE BASIC RULES FOR CHILDREN:

Our children are the continuation of our life and work. We convey to them our whole Psycho-Genealogy along with the burden of inherited beliefs and values that have also been transmitted to us throughout a lifetime.

An harmonious, synergetic, positive and healthy relationship with them is thus fundamental to the integral quality of life, for the whole family.

The *Child Trauma Institute* in Washington has published a few brief references on how to create a healthy relationship with our children and ensure them a good sense of emotional stability. In short they state that,

1. Be an unambiguous reference!
    Respect the archetype: Parents are parents and children are children!
    They expect that a father be a father, and therefore, tell them how, when and who does what. Give them directions by your own example and be supportive.

2. Be consistent!
    If you decide upon something, make it so!
    This applies to rewards and punishments, you should not, however, exaggerate in one case or the other.

3. Be friendly and open, but do not abandon your place as a parent and have fun with them!

Finally, remember to support but not limit them. Children need to experience life, and the sooner they do it, benefiting from a supportive family environment the better they learn and the less painful are the experiences.

CREATIVE AND INHIBITOR POWER OF BELIEFS

Beliefs are generalizations of our perception of the world. That is, they are the on / off switch that allows you to do everything.

During the process of working with your beliefs, it is important to find what your positive ones are (the beliefs that push you towards the desired action) as well as the limiting ones (those beliefs that do not allow you to do what you want).

In the following lines we introduce you some of these beliefs listed from the most external by areas, to the deepest ones,

EXERCISE: *Checking consistency of beliefs*

First: Check List
Complete the following lists with your personal beliefs.

Second: Evaluation
For each one of these beliefs, consider the facts or experiences that you have had that confirm each belief, and those that contradict them.

Third: Consistency
Make your conscious evaluation on each of them to check its consistency.

External environment
- They cannot do that!
- The environment of my neighborhood is not good!
- The house is not big enough!
- With this employment policy I can only be unemployed!
- _____

Behaviors
- I have a fantastic attitude!
- I look like your mother!
- I do not know how to behave in society!
- _____

Capabilities
- I have a knack for decorating!
- I can only make money!
- When someone enters the room I already know problem he has!
- _____

Beliefs and Values
- I believe in you!
- It is not worth the effort!
- Without my family I am nobody!
- _____

Identity: The reference to metaphors, mythology and archetypes, binds us to our identity.
- I am an angel on Earth...
- I am an emperor in this country...
- _____

Spiritual
- It is karma!
- God has forgotten me!
- It is my mission in life.
- Something makes me afraid.
- God meant for me to be sick.
- I remember exactly why I am living this reincarnation!
- _____

EXERCISE: *Limiting beliefs and creative potential*

Identify and write down:

A. The five beliefs that have limited you most in life.
B. The five beliefs that would have helped you the most, if you had them.
C. The main negative and positive belief in each of the Palaces of Feng Shui.
D. Check their consistency as in the previous exercise.

Mansion 8 · Knowledge and Spirituality

Gèn (Mountain)

This trigram figures the Mountain and is associated with the element Earth and the youngest son, and represents the direction Northeast (NE).

The area of knowledge and personal development allow you to improve your heaven luck through spiritual and personal development.

When you are centered, it means that you are aligned with your Mind, Body and Spirit, and it includes the vision you have of the world, selecting the reality you live in based on the mental filters of the brain's reticular formation.

The capacity to accommodate this vision to the reality and the choices you make in your path living your mission, or "personal legend", is an integrant part of a full life and well- being.

There is a hierarchy in the assessment and intervention in life, where each logical level integrates and organizes the operational dimensions of the lower levels, so that a change at a higher level will affect areas in the lower ones, creating a cascade effect top down.

From the most to the least complex, you will find listed below, the seven logical levels of learning, perception and change, as well as the key issues raised in all these dimensions from spirituality to behaviors and their context, and a set of critical questions to highlight these different situations.

The **seven logical levels** of perception and action, from the most complex to the more simple ones are,

1. Spiritual
2. Identity
3. Values
4. Beliefs
5. Skills and capabilities
6. Behaviors
7. Contexts

These levels define for each one of us:

- *To whom / for what?*
  The Spiritual level, refers to a broader dimension of the "I", covering all of our "tribes", family, community, race, nationality, etc.
- *Who?*
  The *Identity level,* refers to the active or inactive being that determines a broader purpose, it confirms and strengthens beliefs and values that give meaning to the "I".
- *Why?*
  The Values and Beliefs level, refers to the inner drivers that support or contradict our capabilities.
- *How?*
  The Skills level, refers to the way we conduct and drive our actions and behaviors according to plan, strategy or mental map that giving it a meaning.
- *What?*
  The Behaviors level, refers to the specific actions and reactions developed in this environment.

- *Where and when?*
  The Contexts, define the opportunities and constraints that we face.

The following **contextual questions** will help you to highlight where you are in every circumstance:

Who?
What is my mission in life?
Why do I do this?
What do I believe and what value does this has to me (what moves and motivates me)?
Do my beliefs and values motivate me?
How do I do that?
Which of my skills rely on my State of mind/Strategies/mental maps?
What do I do?
What behaviors do I adopt to act and react in specific situations?
Where and *when* do I get these actions and reactions?
In which external contexts do I have these behaviors?

Finally, ask yourself:

What skills and behaviors do I still need to acquire to be and to do what is important to me, and different from what I have done so far?

Modern approaches of society, push us to develop excessively the left side of the rational, objective, logical brain, omitting therefore the susceptibility, the global and holistic vision of the right side. Developing and working with both sides of the brain allows us a capacity of full analysis and intervention of it, which is the main target of Brain Yoga or Brain Gym.

Remember also that the left side of the body is governed by the right side of the brain, and conversely, the right side of the brain coordinates the left side of the body.

You can check the consistence between what you are, how you present yourself, and how comfortable you are with it, answering the following questions.

LEFT BRAIN	RIGHT BRAIN
Rational	*Emotional*
Analytical	*Artistic*
Logic	*Global*
Sequential	*Globalized*
Linear	*Metaphoric*
Reflexive	*Musical*
Focus on literal sense	*Creative*
Essentially verbal	*Divergent*
Objective	*Holistic*
Masculine	*Feminine*

You may now, do some exercises for developing the balance between the rational and the emotional area of the brain

Writing or drawing with your left hand, keeping a balanced posture on both sides of the body, supported symmetrically in both legs, describe large 8's or infinity circles with your arms straight,... are some of the exercises that promote this balance.

The four steps of the learning process

Just remember when you first learn to ride a bicycle....

> ➤ I don't know that I don't know
> ➤ I know that I don't know

J.J. Lupi

Now I can start the learning process......

> ➢ I know that I know
> ➢ I don't know (remember anymore) that I know

Which means that finally every,

- Learning
- Behavior
- Change

are ... Unconscious!

Mansion 9 · Self-realization, Image and projects

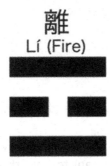

Lí (Fire)

This trigram pictures Fire and is associated with this element, it is the middle child, and represents the direction South (S).

Enlightenment is to find your true personality through personal achievement. Here you overcome the Area 4 of material abundance, to achieve higher goals, and go from Emperor to Pope archetypically speaking.

Consistently connecting and projecting your true essence, showing the higher values of your identity and spirituality are the essence of Mansion 9, related to the opposing mansion of professional career and life projects framing your achievements. This is your projected image.

Self-esteem means to love and value yourself, to be aware of who you are and what it is you aim for; to become consistent! This knowledge and acceptance of yourself, as well as the effort to continue improving, is very different from being presumptuous or selfish.

During this ongoing work of improvement and personal development, always remember to appreciate your results and more obvious qualities, keeping and reinforcing a positive image of yourself.

1. Who am I?
2. What is the meaning of my life and my social connections?
3. How do I feel connected to?
   - What I am...
   - What I believe...
   - What I can...
   - My behavior...
   - Where and with whom and under what circumstances...

You are not what you do, so your Identity is different from your behavior. It is most important to note this distinction when you consider yourself relating to others.

One of the main usual misleading's is to confuse what you are and always will be, with how you behave or what you do, because that you can change and do another thing any time, or choose to do something different.

Some examples of confusion between identity and behavior:

- "I am a fool" instead of "I behaved like a fool".
- "I can't do anything" instead of "I'm out of work".
- "I'm Gay" instead of "I chose to be gay".
- "I am a housewife" instead of "I clean my house".
- "I am a diabetic" instead of "I have type II diabetes".
- "A director does not do certain things" instead of "I have a director's position and my own identity beyond that."
- "I don't do anything right" instead of "I have to learn to work with computers"
- "I am stupid" instead of "I didn't want to study that is why I haven't learned this"
- "I am not educated" instead of "my training does not include a master's degree"
- "I am a bad manager" instead of "I have to study Finances if I have to manage the financial department of the company"

A **practical application**, is when you communicate with others questioning about a process and you use the "why" form, questioning their identity, instead of a more subtle form on "how", which relates to behaviors and is easier to accept and change.

EXERCISE: *Identity and behaviors*

Identify people or situations for which you can confuse their identity with their behavior.

EXERCISE: *Enhancing Self Esteem*

Evaluate if you have a healthy and operational self-esteem by answering the questionnaire that follows:

- Do you accept yourself as you really are?
  This acceptance includes your physical appearance, your emotions and feelings, your weaknesses and strengths.

- Do you value what you do?
  Are you ashamed and respond dodging when someone asks you "what do you do"?

TO BE DONE DURING A THREE WEEKS PERIOD:

Every morning go to the mirror of your bathroom and look deep into your eyes. Say it with conviction, three times out and loud:

"I love and I accept myself exactly as I am!"

Or specify, if you have any particularly sensitive area:

"I accept my _____, and love myself deeply and completely as I am!

Take note of any feeling of discomfort you might find. Repeat this exercise every day for three or more weeks until you no longer feel any discomfort.

Start by doing this exercise while fully dressed and continue until you can do this exercise completely naked in front of the mirror. Take note of the improvements as to its full acceptance.

The risk of perverse perfectionism

Intolerance towards your mistakes or those of others result from the excessive concern with your personal or professional issues, and the assumption that you may always be better.

This is a never ending story and it is usually based on the external dependence on other's opinions to form your own image and identity.

- Who and How evaluates perfection?
- What are the marks and limits of quality?

Avoid being your worst enemy!

Get used to making the most of the situations you live, avoid perfectionism, value each moment as it is.

This healthy consistency improves clearly the energy that you project, so try to enhance yours every day.

Beware of how you communicate. You cannot: NOT communicate. Be it by words, attitudes or nonverbal messages.

Remember: You don't have a second chance to make a first impression!

Mansion 1 · Career, Profession and Life Prospects

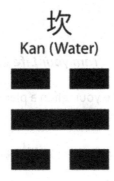

Kan (Water)

This trigram pictures the element Water and is associated with the middle child. It represents the North direction (N).

This mansion is the area of the professional career, based on a life project which should be consistent with the way you live and what you like,, allowing you to connect and project your true essence, that is, the highest value of your identity and spirituality represented in mansion 9 we saw above which is in direct line opposing this mansion.

> *"There is no favorable wind for the sailor who doesn't know where he is heading for!"*

Life Compass and Goals

Often due to emotional states associated with periods of increased stress it is difficult to define goals, and well-formed outcomes. However, you usually have a clear perception of what you like or not.

Through this small exercise you can create a "Directional Compass" that will be a reference chart enabling you to realize whether your decisions keep you "on course" towards the path you have chosen, without conditioning you towards more specific goals.

EXERCISE: *Directions from your Life Compass*

During 60 minutes isolate yourself in a place where you cannot be disturbed.

Get two white sheets of paper, and a blue and red pen.

First 25 minutes, using the color Red,
Write a long list of everything you want to get away from in your life. (Minimum 15 things people or situations.)

Rest for 10 minutes and change the Sheet and the pen to the blue one

Last 25 minutes, using the color Blue,
Write a long list of everything you want to attract to your life (Minimum 15 things, people or situations.)

Usage:

Keep the 2 pages with you.

Take note that every decision you make will bring you closer or take you away from this reference line. Identify and correct the deviations in good time.

The Road to Success is based in five main principles:

1. Know your outcome
2. Have behavioral flexibility
3. Have sensory acuity

4. Always operate with a physiology and psychology of excellence
5. ACT!

EXERCISE: *priority goals*

Write your five priority goals for your life, NOW

Next, give each one a priority and assign them a deadline and an element or evidence, a marker which indicates when you have reached this goal.

	Goal	Deadline	Evidence
1			
2			
3			
4			
5			

Anchors and other unconscious power resources

What is an anchor? This concept comes from Pavlov. Do you remember Pavlov's famous dog?

What Pavlov did to his dogs, was to ring a bell and show the dogs a steak. Repeatedly, he rang the bell and the dogs seeing a steak, of course, salivated.

After a time, he only rang the bell and the dogs salivate, even without seeing any piece of meat. Pavlov deduced through this experiment, the theory of **stimulus - response.**

The sound of the bell was actually an **anchor.**

An anchor exists whenever a person is in an intense state, and at the summit of this psycho physiological experience; a specific stimulus is consistently applied.

The emotional state and the specific stimulus are neurologically linked, making it continuously reproducible when you trigger the same stimulus (anchor).

Anchors are gestures, music, words, looks, touches, and many things that make us feel suddenly, as if transported to other realms, spaces, realities. These anchors can lead us to positive states –the positive anchors – as to the negative states as sadness, depression... - the negative anchors -, so it is important to become aware of their existence and how you use it or protect yourself from them.

An example of an anchor with the negative effects is the hugs of intimacy and demonstration of affection that are often offered in situations of disasters to comfort someone and end up being seen as an anchor which associates hugging with stressful feelings.

EXERCISE: *Identify some of the main anchors of your life:*

My first anchors:

- Where?
- How?
- Why?

Mansion 2 · Relationships, Associations and Partners

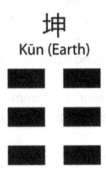

坤
Kūn (Earth)

This trigram represents the element Earth and is associated with the mother archetype and the Northwest direction (NO).

When the air traffic controller gives an instruction to the pilot this one should indicate that he understood the message received from the controller. In most communications, in the context of our relationships, this is not a common procedure, and it is, probably, the main underlying reason of many problems.

Effective communication is the basis of any healthy relationships!

Effective communication implies that you understand that each part involved (the other), has its own perception of reality and all the aspects involving it, which are necessarily different from your perspective, as we saw early in the book.

The respect for each of these individual positions and their expression in terms of agreement and consensus, need to follow some rules,

- Clarifying your position. Each of the parties should speak exclusively about his person, and not get into the other person territory, which will always be perceived as a threat.

- Put yourself in each other's place, to start an agreement rather than a confrontation.
- Do not presume to know (mind reading) the other. Ask what you want to know.
- Do not take anything personally. What others say is only their own projection.
- Use the proper channel of communication. (see below)
- Review the answers you get, and draw your own conclusions.

Some practical exercises to enhance your ability to communicate.

EXERCISE: *Perceptive positions*

This exercise aims to increase your ability to "Put yourself in the place of the other" and communicate your intention to initiate an agreement rather than a confrontation.

What is meant by "Put yourself in the place of the other" can be tested physically. You can understand this, when you change your physical place and go to the usual place of the other party assuming its physical positions and behaviors, as in the exercise that follows.

Think about a situation that you have to deal with someone. Now,

- ➢ Clarify and take notes of your expectations and perceptions of the situation,
- ➢ From the same place try to imagine the expectations and perceptions of the other person,
- ➢ Now move yourself to the other's usual place and assume the physical posture of that person, and think of the situation from its perspective...
- ➢ Finally go back to your initial position and reevaluate the situation. Re-imagine your expectations and perceptions,

...............it was different, wasn't it?

Channels of perception

Another lesser-known reason and one that often prevents your communication skills, concerns the channels of perception. The following example is a familiar scene already known to many people:

The husband says, "Can you hear me?"
The wife replies, "I do not see what you want to tell me!"
The husband returns: "I can repeat slowly what I want!"
The wife replies: "Why don't you show me what you need?"
The son hears this and whispers: "I feel that this is not is going well... "

Reality is created by our brain, interpreting information from our sensory channels - eyes, ears, nose, mouth, skin.

Our five senses are the **only 5 input channels** of your perception of what goes around you. From these 5 sensors, three are considered the main channels, the Visual, Auditory and Kinesthetic (VAK), and the other two (smell and taste) are secondary channels, although very important to capture a full definition of your reality.

From these two, the smell is special, because it is the only one connected directly to the emotional area of the brain.

Your mental models define, how you interpret the actions of another person, and how you act and react in all domains of your life. That is why it is so important to understand these models and become aware of their impact.

EXERCISE: *Perceptions*

1- Identify in the above dialogue, from previous page, the channels used by husband, wife and son.
2- How do you see the woman in next image? Is she young or old?

Depending on how you create our internal representations, you create the world around you.

Yin Yang in your Mind

The Yin Yang in your mind manifests through the balance of Right and Left Brain which are the two parts of the brain with distinct functions, mediated by an area called the Corpus Callosum, acting as a bridge between the other two.

The Left Brain configures our Yang, rational, masculine, and assertive characteristics, while the Right Brain, concerns the Yin side, more feminine, global and emotional, part of our personality.

YIN	YANG
RIGHT BRAIN	**LEFT BRAIN**
Creativity	Diagnosys
Decisions	Processing
Strategicall	Data
Future	Subjects
global	sequencial
implicit	explicit
unconscious	conscious
general	Specific
global	parts
intuitions	cognitions
subtle world	hard facts
associated	dissociated
analogical	digital
Speech	Integral processing
Time Intervals Estimation	Spatial Orientation
Language	Non Verbal Sounds
Reading	Visual-Spatial Capacity
Associative Thinking	Non Verbal Ideation
Calculating	Melodies Recognition
Analitical Processing	Melodies Memorizing
Right Vision	Left Vision
Analitical	(W)Holistic

Fig 23

Each side runs the opposite part of the physical body, so the Right side concerns the left part of the body, as well as the Left brain concerns the right side of the body, except for the ears that are connected with each brain on the same side.

You can identify a more emotional or intellectual response, for example, through the eye more or less opened of the person you are interacting with: if their right eye is clearly more opened, you can figure out they are thinking more than feeling, and if their left eye is clearly more opened then the right one, you have a more emotional than mental response.

Representation Systems and Communication Channels

We have seen so far that reality is not grasped the same way by all people. We can therefore say that the Representational Systems (or Sensory Modalities) are the way your mind encodes information using one or various sensory systems, from the VAKOG:

- V = Visual
- A = Auditory (pure and / or digital audio)
- K = Kinesthetic
- O = Olfactory
- G = Gustative

Although we can all use each and every of these Representational Systems together, the truth is, each of us has a preferential system, or a system we use predominantly to think consciously and thus organize the experience.

In practice, the reality we live in is built through the perception we have of it, filtered by the internal representational systems linked to our five senses, thus generating people more Visual, Auditory or Kinesthetic.

If you access equally all your channels of interaction with the world through all representational systems, the VAKOG senses, you will be more close to fully experience life as an essential part to fulfill and manifest all your creative potential.

EXERCISE: *Your Representational Systems*

Evaluate within your relationships what is the preferred channel of representation of each one, including your own, and try to expand your ways of communication, using more channels than usual.

There are specific words and sentences related with each channel, helping you to accessthe Representational Systems, as we show you below:

Auditory
· Give me your ears
· Shut up
· Ears are full
· I cannot hear anymore
· The main speaker
· Pay attention screaming
· Express yourself clearly
· Listen clearly
· Clearly expressed

Visual
· Eyes full
· Glance
· The naked eye
· Having a perspective
· Of a different color
· Mental Image
· In view of
· To the naked eye
· Short-sighted
· Looking at nothing

Kinesthetic
· All clear
· Put your hands on

- Solid foundations
- Pulling a
  a piece of
  hot argument
- Volatile
- Set the cards on the table
- Do not pursue
- Slip

Now, Complete with your own sentences:

Auditory
-
-
-

Visual
-
-
-

Kinesthetic
-
-
-

The more communication systems you use in the way you communicate, the more people will understand you!

4

"How to do" FENG SHUI YOUR LIFE

The Wheel of Life, a "Matrix for Global Assessment"

First: Evaluate your life structure

From 1-10 (1 being the lowest and 10 highest) the level of satisfaction that you apply to each of the nine areas of your life Ba Gua, represented in the diagram of Fig 18 on chapter 2 above.

Second: Partial assessment of each mansion of life

After this initial Global Assessment we will go into each one of the areas, and check them specifically with some exercises that may help us to improve.

First let's **analyze the status of every mansion**, through the resume below.

For each mansion we analyzed in Part II, starting in number 3 to number 2, we provide you a summary check list for evaluation and Action Plan.

Evaluations should be made through a scale 0 minimum to 10 MAX.

Life mansions:

Mansion 3
How do I deal with my parents?
Am I comfortable with my role on my genealogical line?
How well do I know my family story? Still some secrets?

Mansion 4
How abundant is my life?
How much pleasure is enough for me?
How much do I control my life?

Mansion 5
How is my health?
How is my Wellness?
How do I evaluate (0 to 10), my health & wellness in each level.
  Physical
  Emotional
  Mental
  Energetic
How is the psycho somatic base pattern of my pain or disease?
What is the best new thought pattern to recover from it?

Mansion 6
Who are references as personalities?
Where in my life I feel more supported?
Who are my mentors?

Mansion 7
How satisfactory is my relation with my children?
How do they fit in my genealogic line?
How much freedom and creativity do I have in my life?

Mansion 8
Am I comfortable with the level studies I achieved?

Am I comfortable with my spirituality? What are my daily spiritual routines?

How is my regular up date and knowledge improvement?

Mansion 9
How comfortable I feel with the image projected in my personal environments regarding,
    Home
    Work
    Social
Do I get enough recognition from what I do?
Am I consistent with that Image?

Mansion 1
Do I have plans for my future?
How well am I in the roles I choose for myself?
How much my plans did took into account what I like?

Mansion 2
How comfortable do I feel within my intimate relationships?
How comfortable do I feel within my partnerships?
How easy do I communicate?

Review GLS (Global Life Score):

Now Review and sum up the value of all results for each of your questions, then divide the sum by 34. The resulting figure is the:

Global Wheel of Life Score = _____ / 34 = _____

Third: Preliminary action plan

On the following table, write in the 2nd column, the sentences and the words or images that describe your current situation in relation to things, people and situations in each area or mansion of your life:

Priority Area   **X Current Situation** (words, images and sentences)

_____   **Mansion 3**

_____   **Mansion 4**

_____   **Mansion 5**

_____   **Mansion 6**

_____   **Mansion 7**

_____   **Mansion 8**

_____   **Mansion 9**

_____   **Mansion 1**

_____   **Mansion 2**

Forth: Timing for action

Finally, assign to each area a priority from 0-5 and a deadline for action (days, months or years) in the first column above.

Review:

After going through part III of Personal Feng Shui you should review and integrate the new insights in this plan to adjust it to your heaven's luck and personal profile. You are unique!

PART III

Personal Feng Shui

1   Destiny and Life Path
    Predetermination and free will
    The concept of impermanence

2   Your directions in Life
    Your Gua number and personal directions
    Eight mansions secret formula

3   The I Ching Hexagrams and your life path
    Ancient wisdom and modern science

4   Heavenly guidance for your life
    The I Ching protocol
    Mei Hua Sin I, your life path
    Bai-Yuan Pai, and your daily issues

5   The meaning of the Hexagrams and their evolution
    Hexagrams, concepts and modern interpretation
    Changing lines and specific warnings

6   Life cycles and Pillars of destiny
    Archetypes and personal profiles
    Four Pillars of Destiny
    How to calculate your Pillars of Destiny

7   Relationships and human environment

PART III

PERSONAL Feng Shui

*My Life ends where it began, hopefully with
another level of consciousness!*

Have you noticed that your life is governed by more factors than
those that you control or are conscious aware of?

As in Woody Allen's film: "Match Point". What is the main factor
that causes the ball, swinging over the net of the tennis court, to
fall to one side or the other; making one of the players a winner and
the other a loser?

The main question about predetermination in life, and what part of
life can be influenced through your own free will, is the domain of
Heaven's luck answered and analyzed by the Personal Feng Shui.

The Heavenly factors, include destiny, predetermination, faith, luck
and time, and they highlight the unconscious level and the superior
self, allowing you to understand, influence and make sense of your
life path.

1

Destiny and life path

Predetermination and free will

The Feng Shui traditional concept, illustrates your destiny or life path, based on five "Lots", where in each level your ability to influence your life is more or less limited, according to whether the factors involved concern Heaven, Human and Earthly issues.

Heaven controls the two first factors out of your control and influence, which have the main impact in your life, with a predetermination level around 75%. The other three others conditions left, are the ones affecting around 25%, and is where you may act over, to improve your life.

1: At birth, the first breath of life or the Vital Chi which materializes our purpose in life or our "sacred contract. "

The Psycho Genealogic influence and its timing, together with your life purpose, and the previous experiences of our monad, all come together influencing the gestation period, to prepare the first Chi inhalation, at the moment of birth, materializing your most important characteristics. Time also belongs to Heaven.

2: The "luck" that we afford, according to the acknowledgment that we are more or less fortunate in life.

This is the second level of Heaven's luck, or the predetermination level. Together with the previous point concerning the Vital Chi, they account for around 75% of your life's luck.

What is left is the influence you may have in your life depending on your attitude that impacts around 25% of your faith. These concern the next three areas, related to Earthly and Human factors.

3: *The Feng Shui of your environment, or the harmonization with the energies that surround you, concerns the Earthly dimension.*

The **FENG SHUI**, is the choice of the surrounding energy, with people, things and situations, that represent your personal, work and social life, together with its physical components

4: *Cultivate the human side, your skills and personal energy: physical, mental, energetically and emotional. This all belongs to the Human realm*

Your **personal development** in general, is present in your life style through studies, experiences, and activities that affect your physical, mental, emotional and energy balance

5: *The "good deeds" you do in life selflessly, complete the two last factors involved, also depending on your free will.*

The "**good deeds** " you do to others selflessly, spreading and attracting good energy around you.

Thus, the influence of your attitude, impacts around 15% to 25% of your life, and this influence depends mostly on three areas explained in part I the Feng Shui of your environment, in part II on how you change and your life, and in part III on choosing your relations..

The concept of impermanence

*If everything changes, nothing changes
Something must remain stable
so everything can change!*

Things move! This permanent movement is the basis of life. If it does not move, it is usually dead, so you better learn to love it than to leave it.

Quantum Physics Principle of Indetermination (W. Heisenberg, 1901-1976), states that there is always a margin of uncertainty in human knowledge, so you cannot predict anything exactly because the observer influences what is observed, introducing a variable of indetermination, called the Heisenberg constant.

Every complex situation can be made easy if you analyze it through the concept of **constancy** and **change**, as you are born, you grow up, mature and get old: that is change, although, this sequences follow each other in a constant order, so there is some things that don't change, within the permanent changing process.

This main principle is embedded in the Chinese concept that "if everything changes, nothing changes, so something needs to remain, to allow everything to change", and it is represented through nature cycles at micro level which are more or less stable within other larger cycles.

Sometimes you can find some variation on its elements, as for instance the rhythm of the four seasons that follow each other as the year passes by, is a stable cycle although it can change in the long term, as when the Ice ages where there. Within each season everyday climate is also very unpredictable in its specific variables.

The time cycles can change the Chi or the energy on earth and of the living spaces. These movements are studied in depth in the

Compass and the Flying Stars school of Feng Shui that we will analyze briefly later in this chapter.

The major cycle is an ERA with 180 years, and it is based on 9 phases of 20 years of time, organized in three main periods within each cycle: the Upper Period, the Middle period, and the Lower period, each one with 60 years.

In the actual cycle we are at the second part of the lower period, ruled by number 8, which is about prosperity and good fortune, and the full 9 periods are presented in the following figure.

1 ERA = 180 years		
Phase	*Reigning Number*	Latest years involved
Upper Period		
	1	1864 to 1884
	2	1884 to 1904
	3	1904 to 1924
Middle period		
	4	1924 to 1944
	5	1944 to 1964
	6	1964 to 1984
Lower period		
	7	1984 to 2004
	8	2004 to 2024
	9	2024 to 2044

The next chapters will provide you the tools, awareness and exercises that allow you to access your personal energy namely at Heaven's level:

- Access your origins and life path
- Understand impermanence and the hidden dimensions of life processes

- Evaluate your personal energy levels
- Evaluate the actual phase and actual period you are passing through
- Evaluate your inner Potential, Strengths and Weaknesses
- Get help on evaluating opportunities and threats
- Evaluate your Social Support Network, and family constellations
- Access your life periods and cycles
- Locate best moments for action and windrow, to make the most of opportunities

2

Your Directions in Life

Your Gua Number and life directions
Profiles, numbers, cycles and directions

Numbers have always been subject to scientific and empiric studies and interpretations. In the early ages they were associated with symbols and images, like in Taoism, were the 1 was connected with Heaven and the primal force or CHI, the 2 with earthly issues with its polarity Yin Yang, the 3 with man, issued from heaven and earth (1+2=3), the 4 seasons, the 5 elements, and so on.

The Trigram (Gua) number is also associated with the Lo Shu "Magic Square", and your Life cycles as proposed by the Flying Stars and the Compass Schools of Feng Shui.

This is a key issue for the analysis of your Life Path and Luck, as defined by the Feng Shui approach, and origins of life.

The Mei Hua Sin I hexagram, your personal Trigram, your four Pillars of Destiny, your Star and the Flying Stars Life Cycle, will give you a global and specific inside view on your life allowing you a detached strategic view on most issues you lack of perspective.

All of these tools and protocols will let you in an easy and quick way to have a deeper look at your life patterns and cycles, so to understand and manage the best attitude to face life challenges.

Based on the star number archetypes, we can sense the potential energies of the individual through its birth date, using its location on the Magic Square.

It is not the target of this book to go deeper on this subject but we will provide you with some insights on the most important formulas for the key configurations and their meaning.

Now let's calculate your Gua Number (Trigram)

This number will provide you with your best directions, related to where you should be facing when seating on a meeting table, working, studying, point the head your bed, or even on a romantic dinner table.

The next chart, provides you, the Gua numbers for each year between 1900 and 2050, and is where you should look for your decade and the year of each decade that matches when you were born.

In this chart, according to your sex and year of birth, search your Gua Number, matching your Birth Trigram with all its energetic imprint.

This will gives you access to firsthand information about energetic groups, and how you can profit from its usage in daily life.

There is a feminine Gua that differs from the masculine numbers, and if the Personal trigram is number 5, the one in the center that has no direction, it will change into Western Group for males and females.

This personal Gua is used to determine the four most favorable "lucky" or "unlucky" corners of your home, office or an area of a room, creating better energy in your environment, or to determine your four "Inauspicious" directions.

Your Best Directions GUA number
Masculine & feminine

DECADES	0	1	2	3	4	5	6	7	8	9
YEARS Masc.										
1900	1	9	8	7	6	5	4	3	2	1
1910	9	8	7	6	5	4	3	2	1	9
1920	8	7	6	5	4	3	2	1	9	8
1930	7	6	5	4	3	2	1	9	8	7
1940	6	5	4	3	2	1	9	8	7	6
1950	5	4	3	2	1	9	8	7	6	5
1960	4	3	2	1	9	8	7	6	5	4
1970	3	2	1	9	8	7	6	5	4	3
1980	2	1	9	8	7	6	5	4	3	2
1990	1	9	8	7	6	5	4	3	2	1
2000	9	8	7	6	5	4	3	2	1	9
2010	8	7	6	5	4	3	2	1	9	8
2020	7	6	5	4	3	2	1	9	8	7
2030	6	5	4	3	2	1	9	8	7	6
2040	5	4	3	2	1	9	8	7	6	5
2050	4	3	2	1	9	8	7	6	5	4

DECADES	0	1	2	3	4	5	6	7	8	9
YEARS Fem										
1900	5	4	3	2	1	9	8	7	6	5
1910	6	5	4	3	2	1	9	8	7	6
1920	7	8	9	1	2	3	4	5	6	7
1930	8	9	1	2	3	4	5	6	7	8
1940	9	1	2	3	4	5	6	7	8	9
1950	1	2	3	4	5	6	7	8	9	1
1960	2	3	4	5	6	7	8	9	1	2
1970	3	4	5	6	7	8	9	1	2	3
1980	4	5	6	7	8	9	1	2	3	4
1990	5	6	7	8	9	1	2	3	4	5
2000	6	7	8	9	1	2	3	4	5	6
2010	7	8	9	1	2	3	4	5	6	7
2020	8	9	1	2	3	4	5	6	7	8
2030	9	1	2	3	4	5	6	7	8	9
2040	1	2	3	4	5	6	7	8	9	1
2050	2	3	4	5	6	7	8	9	1	2

Male & Female Best Directions

S

East Group — 4, 9, 3, 1 — 5 Masculine

West Group — 2, 7, 8, 6 — 5 Feminine

N

KUA	S	N	E	W	SW	SE	NW	NE
1	++	+	+++	-	----	++++	---	--
2	---	----	-	+++	+	--	++	++++
3	++++	+++	+	----	-	++	--	---
4	+++	++++	++	---	--	+	-	----
6	----	---	--	++++	++	-	+	+++
7	--	-	----	+	+++	---	++++	++
8	-	--	---	++	++++	----	+++	+
9	+	++	++++	--	---	+++	----	-

Fig 24

Best directions (from Best to 4ᵗʰ Best)

- *"Generating breat":*
  Success, prosperity, vitality, recognition and respect.
- *"Heavenly doctor" :*
  Confidence, security, patience and good health
- *Relationship,s Longevity and Health:*
  Self confidence and reliability, harmony in the family and relationships
- *Development:*
  Original trigram self-element. Promotes peace, fulfillment and creativity. Best for sleeping, study and meditate.

Worst directions (from Least Bad to Worst)

- *Harm:*
  Intermittent frustration and insecurity. Accidents and Mishaps. Best compromise for the sleeping directions if two partners have different Gua groups.
- *Five ghosts:*
  Prejudice from fire, robbery, loss of income, together with quarrels and misunderstanding at home and work.
  Avoid place cooker in this location.
- *Six Killings:*
  Legal and health problems with bad sleeping, dispersion, lethargy, missing opportunities, scandals, prone to addictions.
  Remedy could be drains or storage places in this location.
- *Total loss:*
  Career and finance problems, with poor health with tendency for mental problems, accidents and loneliness feelings

Also you should be sleeping work or seat with your face or head pointing to your birth or Gua directions, or at least one of your good directions

Note: The Gua is related to the Chinese new year, from 5 February to 4 February in the following year, so, if you were born in January or the beginning of February (before the 5th), then you should add 1 year to your year of birth. Like, if you were born in January 1985, it's like you were born in 1984. For more specific days of new Chinese year please check the Chinese calendar information on internet or special publications.

Eastern Group People:
Gua: 1 – 9 – 3 – 4 and number 5 Masculine
Main Lucky directions: E- East, S- South, N- Noth, SE- South East

Western Group People:
Gua: 2 – 6 – 7 – 8 and number 5 Feminine
Main Lucky directions: W- West, NE- North East, NW- North West, SW- South West

Based on this grid each one of us have a specific birth Gua Number that make a first distinction between western and eastern people, connected to their lucky or unlucky directions.

Remember:

When sleeping, eating, doing business, or any other current situation of our daily lives, we should be facing our lucky directions in meetings, working table, or where we point our head during sleeping, and avoid the unlucky directions in this situations.

Eight Mansions secret Formula

In order to calculate your best and less favored directions, we give you next the Eight Mansions Feng Shui Formula.

Start calculating your Personal Trigram.
as we present next referring to the XX and XXI centuries birth dates.

Birth dates are considered belonging to that year only if **born after the 4ᵗʰ February.**

Masculine:
Add then two last digits of your birth year
Reduce from 9
Subtract de rest from 10
Result is the number of your Lo Shu Trigram (Gua).

Feminine:
Add then two last digits of your birth year
Reduce from 9
Add de rest to 5
Result is the number of your Lo Shu Trigram (Gua).

NB1: If they are born between 1rst January and 4ᵗʰ February they belong to the previous solar year, so calculate the sum of two last digits minus 1.

NB2: after 2000 males subtract from 9 and females add to 6

NB3: for males 5 consider Gua 8 and for females 5 comsider Gua 2.

Calculate the group you belong to

East Group:
9 LI, 4 SUN, 3 CHEN, 1 KAN

West Group:
2 KUN, 7 TUI, 6 CHIEN, 8 KEN

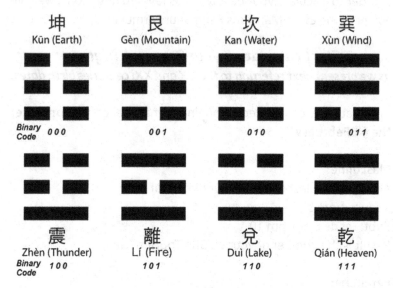

Fig 25
The eight Trigrams and the binary digits

Now calculate your good and worst directions.

Based on the Personal Trigram, change each one of the lines:
Positive Directions: Lines 3, 1-2, 1-2-3, 0
Negative Directions: Lines 1, 2-3, 1-3, 2

<u>*Example:*</u>
Birth year date 1955
Personal Trigram (self-element): 9 (LI)

Change the following lines to calculate directions:

Best directions (from Best to 4th Best)	*Resulting Trigram (Gua)*
3 *Generating breath*	3 (CHEN)
1-2 *Heavenly doctor*	4 (SUN)
1-2-3 *Longevity and Health*	1 (KAN)
0 *Original trigram self-element*	9 (LI)

Worst directions (from Least Bad to Worst)

1 *Accidents and Mishaps*	8 (KEN)
2-3 *Five ghosts*	7 (TUI)
1-3 *Six Killings*	2 (KUN)
2 *Total loss*	6 (CHIEN)

3

The I Ching Hexagrams and your life path

Life is what happens while we are busy making plans!

The I Ching or "Book of Changes" reflects the main concept of "impermanence", where everything is in perpetual movement, but with some underlying order in this movement.

Some of these cycles repeat themselves in the same sequence, like the seasons and the day and night following each other, whether others follow different amplitudes like a hot night and a cold day.

This essential book, is the oldest traditional transmission of knowledge in China, and the only one, common to the two main philosophical traditions: Taoism and Confucionism.

It was produced between 5577 BC and 479 BC, and it is due to the work and findings of Fu Xi (around 5.000 BC), King Wen Wang (1.100 BC) of the Zhou Dynasty, further by his son Zhou Gong and finally by the major Chinese philosopher Confucius (551-479 BC), which retained it as one of the five Confucian Classics: "Shangshu for History, ShiJing for songs, Liji for Rites, and Chunqiu for Spring and autumn annals",

The Emperor Fu Xi, created the trigrams following the assumption of the two forces rolling the Universe, the Yin and the Yang. After that he created the full combination of 8x8 trigrams superposing each one, and give birth to the 64 I Ching Hexagrams.

When he conceived the combination of one trigram over the other, the lower trigram represents the inner or invisible part of the person, thing, or situation, and the upper trigram that represents the external, social, visible part of it.

The sequence of the trigrams are based on the circular graphic representation of FU Xi that is infinite, because you can start at any point and keep turning around in a never ending circle.

Ancient wisdom and modern science

All sequences are based on the Binary numbers used in modern computers, although it was created more than 5.000 years ago.

The I Ching formulas have been used for the development of different sciences and knowledge areas as different as medicine, chi kung, tai chi chuan, astronomy, astrology, decision making processes, Taoist arts, as its most important applications.

Among the original value of this knowledge, is the fact that using modern techniques like binary code from computers, it presents and associates, every subject to the full range of possible approaches and positioning.

The binary language of modern computers with the 0 and 1, is exactly coded in the lines of each of the 64 hexagrams, as you can see in Fig 25, together with the connection with the Atlantis Ring, also illustrated previously in part II.

The secret codex encoded in this ancient knowledge of the I Ching, can be found in its relations with the full Genetic Sequence of the DNA the Book of Life.

Ultimately, life is dependent on the transmission of a genetic code, through the DNA sequence of 4 proteins A, C, G, T, it is proven now, that the changing on the sequence of these proteins on the DNA, can be the only responsible for the difference from a horse, a mosquito and a Human being.

Last but not least we show you the approach to chemical formulations, like the molecules of water, in the following image Fig 26, when considering Oxygen (O) the YANG and Hydrogen (H) as a YIN energy, the water formula can be conceived as the fusion of two energies H2O. These energies are represented by the corresponding continuous and broken lines of the Gua or Trigram Water (KAN).

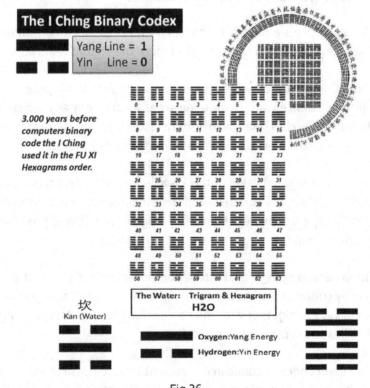

Fig 26
The I CHING Hexagrams and chemical formulas

Even the personal GENEOGRAM, is usually based on the four previous generations which makes 64 ancestors, to reach the deep sources of psycho-genealogic patterns, that are supposed to settle your genealogical patterns line.

The process of consulting the I Ching, had several evolutions along the story but there are two ways known as more effective, that are the mathematical formulas like the MEI HUA SIN, the Bai-Yuan Pai, or the classical use of three coins, or the bamboo sticks throwing.

4

Heavenly guidance for your life

Strategic plans, opportunities, threats and daily issues

The Book of Changes can be consulted for everything in your life, from detailed specific questions about your projects or relations, like what to do about this business opportunity, to general approaches of life issues, like what is the purpose of my being involved in this situation, or how can I find a perfect relationship.

There are a couple of ways to consult this awareness, some based in mathematical calculations, some others based on complex processes supported by bamboo sticks, coins, and lately even with 4 sides bars stamped with each type of character, not to mention the electronic random numbers generators adapted to this purpose.

The typical question for the I Ching is not a Yes or No question, but instead the most useful is the "HOW", type of questions. Understanding the process, which is the how of any issue, will allow you to modify this process, and so change its result.

One of the most consensual rituals for this purpose is explained below and involve 3 old Chinese coins with heads and tails, following this classical and more well-known method, we will use the mathematical approaches to define the hexagram representing your life path, its main purpose and challenges, called the Mei Hua

Sin I, and finally you will learn to use the Bai-Yuan Pai mathematical process for analyzing your daily issues.

The I Ching protocol

The I Ching Hexagrams are the 64 combinations of the basic 8 Trigrams of the BA GUA, and they are composed by an Upper Trigram and a Lower Trigram, where the 6 lines Yin or Yang are counted bottom up.

Each line, depending on their relative position on the hexagram has a special meaning, that may highlight specific issues, as you can see below, from the first lower 3 lines representing your inner potential, from bottom up,

Line 1, is the inner confidence, fear and courage, and knowing your own truth
Line 2, is the inner creativity and intuition, also related to emotions and art
Line 3, is the inner space, the receptivity and acceptance

and the upper lines representing your external issues,

Line 4, is the external security, your professional, financial and material stability
Line 5, is the external creativity, like your personal and social skills, your creative expression
Line 6, is the external space, your Feng Shui and opportunities in life

The I Ching Hexagrams and their structure

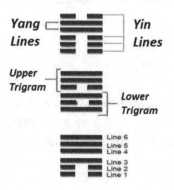

Consulting the "I Ching"

6 is a Yin changing line

7 is a Yang stable line

8 is a Yin stable line

9 is a Yang changing line

Tails   Heads

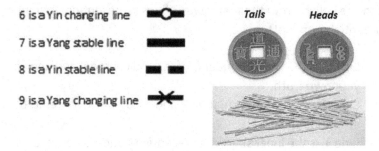

Fig 27
I Ching throwings and interpretation

Consulting the I Ching can be done through several methods from mathematical formulas to dowsing processes using bamboos, sticks, coins, and a variety of systems developed along the years.

Traditionally the Bamboo sticks or the old Chinese coins are used, with Heads and Tails, where **Heads** are considered as odd, yang number **3** and **Tails** considered as even, yin, number **2**, as we show below.

So throwing the 3 coins can sum up from 6 (3X **2**), to 9 (3X **3**), considering the extreme numbers 6 and 9 as unstable lines and the middle numbers 7 and 8 as stable lines.

The unstable lines (6 and 9) will have special meanings and special advices, and beside they will change to their opposite ones (Yin / Yang), creating a new hexagram and announcing an evolution of the changing process.

To launch the consultation:

You should throwing six times the coins and note every time the number resulting from the sum of the three coins, counting 3 for the heads, and 2 for the tails.

So we have the four possible combinations for summing up the value of the 3 coins 6, 7, 8 or 9, as illustrated in image above.

The numbers are noted and represent the six lines from bottom up, and will finally be written as solid lines for numbers 7 and 9, and as broken lines for numbers 6 and 8, as shown in Fig 27 above, keeping in mind that 6 and 9 are changing lines.

After six times throwing the three coins we have six numbers corresponding to 6 lines, which are the superposition of two trigrams with three lines each, resulting in one of the I Ching 64 hexagrams.

To consult the I Ching with one of the processes showed below, and find the specific lines that answer your question, you should,

Take the line 1, 2 and 3 assembled, that constitute the **lower** Trigram
Take the line 4, 5 and 6 assembled, that constitute the **upper** Trigram

J.J. Lupi

Finally,

> Check in the Chart o Fig 29 below, the two Trigrams and find
> out the Number of the **Hexagram** resulting

Each Hexagram is based on two Trigrams one on the top of other,
so the next step is to look in the grid of the Map from Fig 29 on the
Hexagrams, and check the meaning of the Hexagram, resulting
from assembling the lower trigram and the upper trigram, in this
chart.

Now we can look at the main advices and characteristics of the
process, and do not forget to read about the specific significant of
each of the changing lines.

This book present you just a small summary of their significances,
but it is not our aim to go deeper in the details of each subject,
because you can get further information in several sources available.

Last but not least, read the meaning of this hexagram and then
analyse its **evolution** by changing to their opposite every changing
line, which are the lines corresponding to numbers 6 and 9.

This resulting Hexagram will show you the probable direction
where the actual forces are pushing the question at the base of the
consultation.

Mei Hua Sin I, or the Plum Flower Mind I Ching

To evaluate your heaven's life path

Chau Yung, lived in 1000 DC,in the SONG dynasty, and created the method called Mei Hua Sin I (Plum Flower Mind I Ching), as a mathematical approach to form the hexagrams instead of the traditional ways of drawing. This new method is based on objective life events connected with our time and space environment.

There are the **postnatal** and **prenatal** methods of approaching the phenomena. The postnatal method is based on the analysis of nature and energy interactions at the moment and the location of events, and the prenatal uses genealogic type of data to produce the Hexagrams for people things and situations, based on a few mathematical calculations as we will show it hereafter.

Prenatal Formula and meaning (Check from Fig 29):

Upper Trigram = R(U)
Formula: (Y + M + D) / 8 => R
R is the reminder of quotient (from 1 to 7, and If reminder is 0, then use 8)
Y = Year (YYYY) reminder from division by 12 (if reminder is 0, then use 12)
M = Month
D = Day

Lower Trigram = R(L)
Formula: (Y + M + D + H) / 8 => R
R is the reminder of quotient (from 1 to 7, and If reminder is 0, then use 8)
Y = Year (YYYY) reminder from division by 12 (if reminder is 0, then use 12)

J.J. Lupi

M = Month
D = Day
H = Hour based on 24h number, using the number of the beginning
    hour to its end.

Change Line = R(L)
Formula: (Y + M + D + H) / 6 => R
**R is the reminder of quotient (from 1 to 5, and If reminder is 0,
then use 6)**
Y = Year (YYYY) reminder from division by 12 (if reminder is 0,
    then use 12)
M = Month
D = Day
H = Hour based on 24h number, using the number of the beginning
    hour to its end.

<u>EXAMPLE:</u>

Case Study of application of the A MEI HUA SIN I (PLUM FLOWER
MIND I CHING).

Name: Katryn
Date of birth: feb 8, 1979
Hour and location: Europe 11h15m
Let's calculate now:

Upper TRIGRAM = 5 Wind / SUN
    (1979/12) => R=11
    Month: Feb = 2
    Day = 8
    (11+2+8)=21 / 8 => R= **5**

Lower TRIGRAM = 8 Earth / KUN
    Hour 11h15m => 11
    (11+2+8+11)=32 / 8 => R= **0 = 8**

RESULT:

Resulting Hexagram: Hexagram 20,

Description: Contemplation, the Withholding

NB: *as you can read from the I Ching matrix that Fig 29, combining the upper and lower Trigrams, followed by the meaning of the Hexagrams,.*

Changing Line = 2

$(11+2+8+11)=32/6 => R= 2$

Description: To avoid mistakes you should widening your view over the situation. If you look at a room from a semi open door you cannot see all that there is inside.

Post Heaven BA GUA	6	7	9	3	4	1	8	2
Nr.	1	2	3	4	5	6	7	8
KUA or TRIGRAM	乾 Qián (Heaven)	兌 Duì (Lake)	離 Li (Fire)	震 Zhèn (Thunder)	巽 Xùn (Wind)	坎 Kan (Water)	艮 Gèn (Mountain)	坤 Kūn (Earth)
Mei Hua Sin I	1	2	3	4	5	6	7	8 or 0
Bai-Yuan Pai	8 or 0	7	6	5	4	3	2	1
Nature	Heaven	Lake	Fire	Thunder	Wind	Water	Mountain	Earth
Name	CHIEN	TUI	LI	CHEN	SUN	KAN	KEN	KUN
Element	Metal	Metal	Fire	Wood	Wood	Water	Earth	Earth
Concept	Creator	Serenity	Adherent	Promoting	Penetrating	Abyss	Imobiling	Receiver
Direction	SW	W	S	E	SE	N	NE	NW
Color	WHITE	WHITE	RED	GREEN	GREEN	BLACK	TERRACOTA	YELLOW
Months	October	Aug. Sept.	May. June	March - April	April - May	Nov.-Dic.-Jan.	January - Feb.	June - July
Animal	DOG - PIG	ROOSTER	HORSE	RABBIT	DRAGON-SNAKE	RAT	OX	SHEEP
BINARY DIGIT	111	110	101	100	011	010	001	000

TRIGRAMS from Post Heaven Ba Gua and their conections

Fig 28
The Trigrams sequences of early and later heaven

Finally, to get a more complete view on any question you may create the Hexagram representing the final situation of the issue. To do this, you just move the changing line of your original Hexagram to its opposite, i.e. if it is a Yin Line you change it to a Yang line, and if it is a Yang line you change it to a Yin line.

Then you can check the probable ending of the situation by reading the meaning of the hexagram resulting.

Example:

In the previous case, changing the line 2, will transform Hexagram 20 (withholding) in Hexagram 59 (dispersing)

For approaching the active phase of resolving the same issue you may derive another Hexagram, or the middle one, by superposing an outer Trigram made by lines 3, 4, 5, to an Inner Trigram made by lines 2, 3, 4 of the original Hexagram. The resulting Hexagram will illuminate the process of the active phase of the issue.

Example:

In the previous case, will transform Hexagram 20 (withholding) in Hexagram 23 (vulnerability).

These could mean for a Life Journey, that from a first phase of withholding (H20) with some limitations, you will pass through a period of vulnerability (H23) during the active phase, before being able to disperse (H59) and communicate your ideas.

The Bai-Yuan Pai and your daily issues

Mathematical formula method to assess your daily issues

Used for highlighting unconscious responses to daily issues, this method is dated around the year 1100 of our era, is based on the Early Heaven Ba Gua, with the following **Trigrams** sequence:

TRIGRAM NUMBER,

1. **KUN - Earth**
2. **KEN- Mountain**
3. **KAN - Water**
4. **SUN - Wind**
5. **CHEN - Thunder**
6. **LI - Fire**
7. **TUI - Lake**
8. **CHIEN- Heaven**

NB. If reminder equals 0 then use Trigram 8.

This is done by the practitioner after writing his question, asking the client to throw some unconscious numbers, with at least three digits.

The first sequence will provide the Upper Trigram and the second sequence providing the Lower Trigram.

The process to generate the number of each trigram is as follows,

> **You say your number with more than three digits**
> **Divide this number by 8**
> **Calculate the reminder: this is the number of your Trigram**

Example:

Question? "How should I manage the project I am working on?

First number: 435

435 / 8 => Reminder = 3

Second Number: 9238

9238 / 8 => Reminder = 6

RESULTING HEXAGRAM (from Fig 29):

Trigram (3) Water over Trigram (6) Fire results in

HEXAGRAM number 63 "After completion"

Small and timely actions. If you act too late disorder comes. Extraordinary diplomatic behavior is demanded here to keep everything we already achieved. Furthermore you should prudent and try to anticipate any unpredictable event, to be ready for it.

This process can be used easily for most life questions, and the interpretation should be done according to the strategically or operational level of the issue.

5

The Meaning of the hexagrams and their evolution

Every hexagram we saw before, is build up with six lines, some stable ones and some unstable, that will show us the dynamics involved in every situation consulted. For the purpose of this book we will stay on this level of analyses, so if you want to go further, you can consult our website, or any other material specific to the I Ching, hexagrams.

Besides, the main meaning of the Hexagram and its application for each area of life, there are specific information based on the changing lines and its evolution. Also for deeper development, we can analyze the inside trigrams and their reverse, in order to understand the occult inner forces driving every issue.

When there is an evolutionary process involved, from the first hexagram, you can derive two others: one to illustrate the final result of the process, and the other to illustrate the action during the development of the issue.

To illustrate the action and the development of the process, you create another hexagram based on the first one using lines 2, 3 and 4 to build up the new lower Trigram, and lines 3, 4 and 5 to build up the new upper Trigram.

J.J. Lupi

To overlook the final result of the process, you create another hexagram by changing to their opposite any changing line of the base Hexagram, so any Yin changing line will become a Yang line and any yang changing line will become a Yin line in the ending resulting hexagram.

You should note that the hexagrams are arranged in a way that each one of the energies is followed by its opposite, as for example the Hexagram 1 "Heaven", where each line or YAO is a Yang line, is followed by the Hexagram 2 "Earth", composed only by Yin or interrupted lines, in a way that bring the opposite views gathered together, to enlighten the shadow side of each question.

Let's for the moment have a first look on the Hexagrams Matrix, where you can find their number from the two constitutional upper and lower trigrams, and then we will present you summary of their meaning and general recommendations.

TRIGRAM Upper → Lower ↓	qián Heaven	zhèn Thunder	kǎn Water	gèn Mountain	kūn Earth	xùn Wind	lí Fire	duì Lake
qián Heaven	1	34	5	26	11	09	14	43
zhèn Thunder	25	51	3	27	24	42	21	17
kǎn Water	6	40	29	4	7	59	64	47
gèn Mountain	33	62	39	52	15	53	56	31
kūn Earth	12	16	8	23	2	20	35	45
xùn Wind	44	32	48	18	46	57	50	28
lí Fire	13	55	63	22	36	37	30	49
duì Lake	10	54	60	41	19	61	38	58

Fig 29
The I Ching map of the hexagrams

In the following pages you can find a brief summary of the main significance of each hexagram, in order to allow you to have a first glance on your life issues, in the light of this ancient knowledge. Further, we will analyze in the annex in the end of the book, one full comment real story, on the life path represented by the hexagram energies, with a case study based on the life challenge Hexagram calculated through the MEI Hua SIN I method.

Hexagrams Concepts and Modern Interpretation

Hexagram 1 – Qian - Heaven, the power of creation
Force, the Creative, Possessing Creative Power & Skill

To attain your targets, show calm and patience, your huge inner capacity allow you to proceed in any direction, so you just need to respect the natural rhythms of things and do not rush. Your success will be granted if you proceed this way.

Hexagram 2 – Kun - Earth, the receptive natural answer
Field, The Receptive, Following guidance and subtle action brings good fortune; Needing Knowledge & Skill; Do not force matters and go with the flow

Everything will arrive at the right moment, so you better not act in this moment. Follow stronger people with more decision making capacity, with humility and strong will force. Be aware and listen to your inner and psychic wisdom, which is better than your rational mind.

Hexagram 3 – Tun - Difficulties at the beginning
Sprouting, Difficulty at the Beginning, Perseverance

Do not worry about any problem, just look for the people that can help you and do not isolate yourself. Be sure you will thank them well.

Hexagram 4 – Meng - Inexperience and the youth
Enthusiasm, Youth foolishness, Enveloped and Inexperienced

Postpone your projects until you have more information's or get the skills needed. Respect the rules and be true even to yourself.

Hexagram 5 – Xu - The waiting
Attending, Waiting, Non Involvement (Wait for now), Progress, Nourishment

Do not initiate anything now, wait for an natural event to happen, but do not fall into laziness, keep your mind fully awake to act in the right moment.

Hexagram 6 – Song - The conflict
Arguing, reunion, Engagement in Conflict

Avoid any controversy, and do not let yourself in a position that makes you enter in any discussion, and if that is impossible manage to settle them quickly. Evaluate how you could reorganize yourself and reconsider your positions if they create huge disturbances.

Hexagram 7 – Shi - The collective force
Leading, the Army, Bringing Together, Teamwork

Try to find the hidden aspects that may be the strongeest and most dangerous of all. Act with awareness and decision. You should consider consulting other people that you are sure to be trustful if you cannot fully trust your own willpower and self-reliance.

Hexagram 8 – Bi - The union
Grouping, Holding Together, Union, Humility

There is nothing negative or definitive. Check the details though the advice of the changing lines of the hexagram and consult again the I Ching in a couple of days.

Hexagram 9 – Xiau Chu - The power of the weak
Small Accumulating, Stillness, Small Taming, Accumulating Resources

Be sincere and confident. Accept small gains or going through an unproductive period. Act with rectitude and show the best of your character, this will be the best attitude against higher forces. Courtesy is the best weapon against prepotency.

Hexagram 10 – Lu - The conduct
Treading (Conduct), Difficulty, Continuing with Alertness

To overcome difficulties, act straight and without double face. Be simple and friendly, avoiding pride. Try to find out how to stay near the source of your problems so you can solve them as soon as the opportunity arises

Hexagram 11 – Tai - Peace and prosperity
Pervading, Peace, Continuous progress

Very favorable period but you should be awake and ask for the best. Be honest.

Hexagram 12 – Pi - Stagnation
Obstruction, Standstill, Small excess

You should beware and distrust, on every issue from work, finances and feelings. Keep even your friends at a certain adequate distance.

Hexagram 13 – Tong Ren - The community
Concordant People, Fellowship, Partnership.

Be more open and friendly to others. Organize something with someone close to you. Avoid egocentrism and lack of connection to others.

Hexagram 14 – Da You - Wealth
Great Possession, Independence, Freedom,

Be correct in your action, use modesty and follow your intuition seeing the good side in everything the surrounding you.

Hexagram 15 – Qian - Modesty
Humbling, Being Reserved, Refraining

Use your auto discipline, and rest quiet in the middle of the multitude. If you want something you can get it but you should disappear and pass unnoticed and discrete.

Hexagram 16 – Yu – Pleasure, harmony and enthusiasm
Providing, Enthusiasm, Inducement, New Stimulus

Calm yourself with some relaxing music, enhance your intuition and remember your parent's longer experience.

Hexagram 17 – Sui - Following
Continuity, adaptation and perseverance

Be useful and keep your targets high. Get around with optimistic and even young people but input some wisdom bases. You will become their leader. Be pure and flexible.

Hexagram 18 – Gu – Poisoning, The decline
Corrupting, Work on the Decayed, Repairing things

Watch out your situation that is already much deteriorated, and find a way to solve it. You are still in time to correct the errors committed not only by yourself but also your family.

Hexagram 19 – Lin - Approaching Greatness
Approach, Approaching Goal, Arriving

Remember that when things go very well at all levels, things may also change, so now is the moment to protect everything and do not forget anything, this way you will not see things worsening

Hexagram 20 – Guan - Contemplation and vision
Viewing, Contemplation, Withholding

Act based on calm, ponder all issues, and remember to take advice from competent people, and by the same way be sure to give advice to others only when you are fully aware of the subject. Our personality will remain untouchable.

Hexagram 21 – Shi He – Punishment, bite and gnawing
Gnawing and Bite, Biting Through, Deciding

You should be decisive and find the root cause of the problem. Cut it clear and net. Do not use palliative solutions-

Hexagram 22 – Bi - Beautiful shape
Adorning, Grace, Embellishing

Enjoy the small daily events without pretending for the moment, any changes in our life. Don't lose your friendly attitude and take care about your good looking to produce a good impression on others. This will set the bases for a better future.

Hexagram 23 – Bo - Stripping
Vulnerability, Stripping, Splitting Apart, Flaying

Hold on and wait for the difficulties to go away. Actually any action from you would be useless. All you can do for the moment is to be generous and make some sacrifices towards someone that may help or comfort you.

Hexagram 24 – Fu - Returning
Turn on circumstances

All difficulties that had blocked you will present a fortunate change now. Keep your faith. Have confidence but keep a wise and intelligent attitude under any circumstances.

Hexagram 25 – Wu Wang – Innocence, without embroiling
Innocence, Without Rashness

Honesty and respect. Be consistent with your pure inner truth and fight adversity with your moral integrity, so you will overcome all difficulties.

Hexagram 26 – Da Chu - Great Accumulating
Great Taming, Accumulating Wisdom

You should valorize your past experiences to understand the root cause and the essence of your problems. Long term project are more favored then short term ones. You should decide the moment to act very carefully.

Hexagram 27 – Yi - Swallowing
Mouth Corners, Seeking Nourishment

Some suffering has brought you the need maybe even unconscious for rest and regenerate yourself and your strength. This nutrition may range from physical to spiritual needs. It can be a need for nutrition as well as a need to nurture others.

Watch out for what you absorb and what you give. Be sure that it corresponds to real needs and valuate this needs with accuracy.

Hexagram 28 – Da Guo - Great Exceeding
Great Preponderance, Great Surpassing

You should learn to know yourself and your true possibilities to avoid major errors. All this situations involve difficulties. Solve then quickly using common sense.

Hexagram 29 – Kan – Abyss, water flow
Moving water, the Abysmal Water, Darkness, Gorge

Even if the situation is difficult you should not renunciate to act upon it. You should profit from this experience to make the useful moves and profit from the least opportunity. Be prudent with people that you surround yourself.

Hexagram 30 – Li – Brightness, Burning flame
The Clinging, Radiance, Attachment

Very positive and enlighten, it involves the risk of excessive passion in all manifestations. You should balance and evaluate with awareness what is really fair, so you will be able to run things as you wish.

Hexagram 31 – Xian – Influence, conjoining
Influence, Attraction

Very important to learn to live with other people, because everyone from the most humble to the most powerful as something to teach you. You should accept whatever destiny reserves to you, but give the best you can so you don't lose these destiny chances.

Hexagram 32 – Heng - Persevering
Duration, Perseverance

Constancy in all situations even if you need to be flexible in some situations but should always keep in mind your personal goals. Rigidity can only raise obstacles, but an adequate answer may help you in any circumstances.

Hexagram 33 – Dun – Hiding, retiring
Retreat, Withdrawing

Actual circumstances do not favor us at all, so it is better to abandon and retreat. Beware to the people that surround you and consider even to cut clear all connections with them.

Hexagram 34 – Da Zhuang - Great Strength
Great Power, Great Boldness

Very positive, but as when things are working well you may tend to push them too much, the advice is to proceed easy going and behave totally correct.

Hexagram 35 – Jin – Advance, secure prospering
Progress, Expansion, Promotion

Everything you must do should be crystal clear without any subterfuge or hidden issues or agreements. Your goals are about to come true but you should pursue a continuous activity to set up a solid base for it.

Hexagram 36 – Ming Yi - Brightness hiding
Darkening of the Light, Brilliance Injured

When anything you may do will come out wrong, you should behave serious and responsible. Don't show your personal qualities because at this stage they cannot be understood, and keep safe your integrity.

Hexagram 37 – Jia Ren - The Family circle
Dwelling People

Behave and respect all members of your family and groups you belong to. This is the only way to favor peace, stillness and the development of your global interests. This hexagram is better for women then for men.

Hexagram 38 – Kui – Strange, contrasts
Unusual Circumstances, Opposition, Division, Divergence

This conflicting situation is wasting your energy. In such cases the only thing you can do is to have patience to face the problems. Avoid alliances with others because you could attract non adequate partners.

Hexagram 39 – Jian - The obstacles
Obstruction, Halting, Hardship

Revise totally your behavior. Even if you do not like it you should admit you were wrong somewhere. Reconsider carefully your targets because surely they are above our strengths.

Hexagram 40 – Jie – Loosen, liberation
Deliverance, Taking-Apart, Solution

You need to decide to put an end to things that are confusing. Maybe you should bury some untruths or presumable errors that have been haunting you. This way you will be able to take control of your life again and make a real turn on to your purposes.

Hexagram 41 – Sun - Diminishing
Decrease

Take it easy and keep calm in any situation, accept small losses and restrictions, because from this will emerge your full recovery. Introduce some changes in your lifestyle to live an healthier life.

Hexagram 42 – Yi - Augmenting
Increase

J.J. Lupi

While in this favorable period you should be responsible and build a solid life, so you will be able in the future to overcome periods of lows and highs in your life. Check your conscience to correct bad behaviors.

Hexagram 43 – Quai – Decision, excess
Define Goals, Breakthrough, Separation, Parting

Erase and restart even if it costs you some sacrifices. You should know that if you will show out your capabilities, you could solve the problems without major efforts.

Hexagram 44 – Gou - Encounter
Coming to Meet, Coupling

Make detailed analysis of the situation and project it in the future, it would hardly be favorable. Everything regarding the feminine people, things and situations is not positive.

Hexagram 45 – Cui - Clustering
Gathering Together, Association, Companionship

Even if you path is smooth and without difficulties, unexpected events may arise. Be ready for this eventuality having all your weapons prepared and ready. This behavior will bring you inner and out peace.

Hexagram 46 – Sheng - Ascending
Pushing Upward, Growing Upward

Don't rush to get what you want, neither sleep over your gains. This message urges you to maintain a constant effort to reach success, accumulating further experiences and small successes, until you have created a solid and indestructible base.

Hexagram 47 – Kun - Confining
Oppression, Exhaustion

This is not a very tranquilizing message. You should be prepared to ride the ups and downs of the waves of life. Be sure to be well anchored in your solid bases.

Hexagram 48 – Jing – The Well
The Rising, Replenishing, Renewal

Look inside yourself, in the deep of your soul to access the emergence of your inner wealth, even if this causes you some kind of suffering.

Hexagram 49 –Ge - Mutation
Revolution, Abolishing the Old

Be prepared to accept sudden changes, like a lightning bolt in a clear sky "the Uranus effect". Be sure that everything to come, even if it worries you, was set up in your destiny and prepared by previous events.

Hexagram 50 – Ding - Holding
The Cauldron, Establishing the New

Set yourself objectives other than economic or earthly pleasures. Develop some activities to develop you psychic and physically, like Yoga, Chi Kung, and learn some purifying techniques.

Hexagram 51 – Zhen - Thunderstorm
Arousing, Mobilizing, Shake

Everything can happen from accidents to change of social condition. Trust your moral integrity, and your resilience, to allow this huge experience to result in a positive and fructifying one.

Hexagram 52 – Gen - Immobility
The Keeping Still

You should stop even if you have problems to face. Time will tell you when the moment to proceed your path is. For the moment avoid any initiative if you want to stay in peace with yourself and others. Just relax, live a tranquil and easy life and use it to make a deep inner search.

Hexagram 53 – Gian – Infiltrating
Development, Auspicious Outlook, Gradual progress

You are in a period of improvement in all areas and soon you will reach your goals. Just keep a respectful behavior and avoid egoism, to reach triumph.

Hexagram 54 – Gui Mei - Converting the Maiden
The Marrying Maiden, Marrying

You should be aware of impermanence of things, and behave in consequence. There is always a beginning and an end. It is useless to fight against it, as recognized by the superior man.

Hexagram 55 – Feng - Abundance
Goal Reached, Ambition Achieved

Even if everything looks fine you should not be to optimistic neither sleep over the previous conquests. Life is as it is and it has its natural cycles, so the only thing you can do is to think about it and take some precautions. You can't do nothing against it.

Hexagram 56 – Lu - The traveler
The Wanderer, Travel, Sojourning

Unstable situations or unawareness may put in danger all you already reached. End your current fights and conflicts, and analyze your behaviors to get over things.

Hexagram 57 – Xun - Subtle Influence
The Gentle, Wise Councel, Ground

Be gentle with everybody, accept things with simplicity and avoid tensions. Get support if needed from someone that can see further then ourselves and that actually as more power or strength

Hexagram 58 – Dui - Joyfull, serenity
The Joyous, Open Influence

Behave with moderation in all aspects of your life. Serenity, controlled joy, sober pleasures, methodical work, select your friendships carefully and with similar tastes and behaviors.

Hexagram 59 – Huan - Dispersing
Dispersion, Dispersal

Learn how to open yourself to others, and get over egoism and unconsidered actions.

Hexagram 60 – Jie – Regulations, limitation
Articulating, Limitation, Discipline

Common sense e and moderation, without applying useless restrictions. Find a way of life where duties and rights are clearly defined, so you will avoid major errors.

Hexagram 61 – Zhong Fu - Inner truth
Staying Focused, Avoid Misrepresentation, Centre Confirming

You should be totally convinced of what you intend to do, as the only way to obtain what you desire. Try to get an objective view instead of only one egoistic perspective.

Hexagram 62 – Xiao Guo - Small Exceeding and extraordinary
Small Preponderance, Small Surpassing

Restriction everywhere. This will lead you to your target results in any field. There are more beautiful, important and pleasant things, but for the moment you should stay with some smaller and not so nice ones.

Hexagram 63 – Ji Ji - Already Completed
After Completion, Completion

Small and timely actions. If you act too late disorder comes. Extraordinary diplomatic behavior is demanded here to keep everything we already achieved. Furthermore you should prudent and try to anticipate any unpredictable event, to be ready for it.

Hexagram 64 – Wei Ji - Not-Yet Completed
Before Completion, Incompletion

No profit until the end, and yet nothing is ever completed. Be very careful, cautious and detailed elaborating your projects. Be cautious and be sure that you have all support, time and inner peace that you need, because if any one of these are missing our efforts will be in vain with all the inevitable consequences.

Changing lines and specific warnings

Every Yin or Yang line can be originated from number 9 (Yang Yang), number 7 (Yin Yang), number 8 (Yang Yin) and number 6 (Yin Yin), with the 6 and 9 representing the extreme Yin and extreme Yang. These extreme numbers 6 and 9, will announce some changes in the situation ... *in the deepest Yang appears the Yin...* and these are called the changing lines.

To analyze further the probable development you should create another Hexagram by transforming every changing line in their opposite, in order to get another Hexagram meaning the evolution of the previous one, and the probable ending situation, as you can see in the example of the Bai-Yuan Pai calculation.

To complement this analyzes please refer to the specific meaning of each of the changing line with specific advices to the issue consulted. This you can do through our website, where you will find access to detailed information on these subjects, beyond the scope of this book.

6

Life cycles and Pillars of destiny

The I Ching approach to the energetic life cycles, is a direct result of the Chinese school, based on Confucius and the TAO of Lao Tsé. This eastern philosophical school integrated the body and mind practices like, Yoga, Meditation, Medicine, and it's an evidence based practical approach. This is one reason how it as survived and its accuracy been proved like no other, along more than 4.000 years as it is the case of the Acupuncture practice.

The gateway for the Universal CHI to enter our galaxy, according to the ancient oriental philosophers, is a specific group of 9 stars at the origin of the Feng Shui School of the Flying Stars. These stars are the 7 stars constellation of the Great Bear, Polaris the brightest star of the Little Bear constellation with pure Yang energy, and Vega representing the pure Yin energy.

The magnetic fields acting over our solar system, our planet and our life's, move according to the changing repetitive cycles of the position of these stars. Over endless observations these energies were associated with some patterns and events that allowed the ever changing evolution of life on earth.

Every one of these stars have been associated with numbers according to the Lo Shu Square and the Trigrams of the Pa Gua of Later Heaven. So the Flying Stars 9 numbers, are represented by the 9 numbers of the LO SHU, and also correspond to the 8

Trigrams of the PA Gua, plus it's center "the TAI CHI" with the Yin Yang symbol, associated with number 5.

Activating or Reducing the energies of these star numbers, is mostly done based on the usage of the cycle of the 5 elements, to foster, controlling or reducing each one, based on the production and control cycles they related to.

To the purpose of the Flying Stars energy we only consider the Yang or Masculine KUA number of the Year, as we will see later on.

Archetypes and personal profiles

Since all ages archetypes, where the soul memory of humanity, reflecting all the concepts that we already know before they were explained to us.

Several approaches of human nature, propose a typology associated with some standard characteristics for each group. Prior to the main psychological archetypes of Carl Jung, to the Eneagram or the Time Line Therapy or NLP classifications, the Feng Shui proposes 12 different profiles associated with your birth date.

The energies and personal profiles presented by the calculations that follows, are based on the two schools, Pillars of Destiny and Flying Stars. They also belong to the Human profiling essays common to large number of psychological schools of personality analysis well known today.

Personal profiles, branches and destiny

These different types of human nature are based on a complex system of 10 Heavenly stems, with 5 elements and 12 earthy branches, within a basic cycle of 60 years (12 X 5= 60).

The first important information about each individual person, things or situations is based on the **Lunar Calendar** and the 12 energies of the earthly branches, also called the 12 animals.

As most peasants and farmers at the time used to notice the rhythms of nature by crop growing and animal activities, the Emperor from HAN dynasty, in the beginning of this era, choose to name the year cycle based on animals in order to facilitate their understanding by peasants.

A more socially contextualized version, stated that the origin of the animal signs is based, on the connection each one have with the seasons and the compass directions for the cardinal points.

The 12 animals for the Chinese zodiac must have been developed in the early stage of Chinese civilization for hundreds of years until it become the current edition; and it's very hard to investigate the real origin.

The mythology attributes to the Buda calling for all animals to meet him before his departure from earth. Only 12 attended the call, whether during the travel some adventures shaped future relations between them.

The folkloric origin of each animal and its position number within the 12, will help us to understand the characteristics and relationships between them. Lord Buda, named each year according to one from the 12 animals following their order of arrival, starting with the Rat and ending with the Boar, because t*he Jade Emperor had decreed that the years on the calendar would be named for each animal in the order they arrived to the meeting*

Named "The Great Race", is the *story highlighting not only the relationships between animals and their human natures, but also their main personalities.*

To reach the local decided by Buda, all animals had to cross a river to arrive to the meeting place where he was waiting.

The Rat decided that the best and fastest way to cross the river was to hop on the back of Ox. The Ox, being naïve and good-natured, agreed to carry him across, but then, as the Ox reached the other side of the river, the Rat jumped ahead and reached the shore first. So he was the first in the competition and of the zodiac.

Following closely behind was strong Ox who was named the 2nd animal in the zodiac. After Ox, came Tiger explaining to Lord Buda, how difficult it was to cross the river with the heavy currents pushing it downstream all the time. But with its powerful strength, Tiger made to shore and was named the 3rd animal in the cycle.

Then the Rabbit arrived, explaining that he crossed the river, jumping from one stone to another and he almost lost the race, but was lucky enough to grab hold of a floating log that later washed him to shore. For that, it became the 4th animal in the Zodiac cycle.

In 5th place was the Dragon that explained that he had to stop and make rain to help all the people and creatures of the earth, and therefore he was held back. Then, on his way to the finish, he saw a little helpless Rabbit clinging onto a log so he did a good deed and gave a puff of breath to the poor creature so that it could land on the shore.

Suddenly, a galloping sound was heard, and the Horse appeared, but, hidden on the Horse's hoof was the Snake, whose sudden appearance gave the Horse a fright, thus making it fall back and giving the Snake the 6th spot, while the Horse placed 7th.

Not long after that, a little distance away, the Goat, Monkey, and Rooster came to the shore. These three creatures helped each other to get to where they are. The Rooster spotted a raft, and took the other two animals with it. Together, the Goat and the Monkey cleared the weeds, and finally got the raft to the shore. Because of their combined efforts, they were named, Goat as the 8th creature, the Monkey as the 9th, and the Rooster the 10th.

The 11th animal was the Dog. Although he was supposed to be the best swimmer, he could not resist the temptation to play a little longer in the river. Finally with his typical noise, the Pig arrived late because he got hungry during the race, promptly stopped for a feast and then took a nap falling asleep. After the siesta, the Pig continued the race and was named the 12th animal of the zodiac cycle.

As a curiosity, it tells about the relations between Cats and Rats; as the worst swimmers in the animal kingdom, and both quite intelligent together with the Rat, the Cat had decided to hop on the back of Ox, and the Ox agreed to carry them both across. Midway across the river, Rat pushed Cat into the water, and arrived first as we saw before. The Cat drowned only arrived in 13th place and did not make it in the zodiac. It is said that that is the main reason why Cats always chase Rats.

Even Countries and Nations have their earthly branch, like China 1949 is an OX, Hong Kong a Tiger, or France as Dog, and the USA Monkey, or the late Russia Federation as a Sheep, based on their birth date or independence day, or even through the geographical world map of each animal birth zone.

To allow us to have some guidance and references of our specific basic nature and for the purpose of this first approach, we are going to present a simplified system to access the basic energies and the life cycles involved.

The Lunar calendar is composed of 4 seasons of 72 days with an inter season of 18 days. The 4 seasons correspond to each one of the four elements – wood, fire, metal, water -, and the inter season period, corresponds to the element earth.

Pillars of Destiny and the eight characters

The main character of each pillar is its "Branch" or animal sign that is then balanced on its earthly expression by the corresponding "Stem".

The Animal ruling your **birth year** is called the "animal hide in your heart", and is the one that most influence your life. There is another animal with huge influence that is the one ruling your **birth hour,** which is called your eastern ascendant, and influences the expression of your Inner Animal in your daily life.

The 24 hours of each day are divided into periods of 2 hours ruled by one animal sign also, starting with the rat between 23h and 1h am, and changing every 2 hours, to end with the Boar between 21h and 23h.

So we have the **Four Pillars of Destiny,** constituted by eight Characters (Ba Zhi) or characteristics that include the yearly animal and stem, the earthly branch and stem for the hour, Month and Day.

Every each one of this Pillars have one Animal, or *"Earthly Branch",* associated together with an element combined with a Yin or Yan Characteristic, which is the *"Heavenly Stem"*. The relative force of each Pillar depends on its strength and harmony of the balance between Stems and branches through their respective compatibility.

We need to take into consideration that the Lunar calendar starts with the Chinese new year, with a first month starting between end January and mid-February (for example, in 2013 it started the 11 February), usually we take the February 5, as the first day of the lunar calendar for practical reasons.

The full cycle of Chinese lunar cycle combines the 12 animals with the five elements in a 60 years period (12x5=60).

Finally the significance of the Four Pillars is summarized below:

> The **Year Pillar**, correspond to your main life energy, and the expression of the self. It is the Yang of the Yang, and sometimes associated with grandfather and ancestors.
>
> The **Month Pillar**, corresponds to the hidden issues from social behavior, or the Yin of Yang
>
> The **Day Pillar**, refers to natural self as presented in your inner circle or the Yang of the Yin ·
>
> The **Hour Pillar**, means your secret garden, or your inner primal impulses, the Yin of the Yin

Four Pillars of Destiny

The *"Four Pillars of destiny"* are the main characteristics of the Feng Shui human typology. Also called *"Bā Zì"* (八字), or Eight Characters because each of the four pillars representing the year, month, day, and hour of one's birth, is represented by two characters; one character for a *Heavenly Stem* and one character for an *Earthly Branch*.

The zodiac of twelve animal signs represents twelve different types of personality. The 12 zodiac animal reference is a folkloric representation of the 12 Earthly Branches. The zodiac traditionally begins with the sign of the Rat, and the following are the twelve zodiac signs in order and their characteristics.

Each of the 12 animals are governed by an element plus a Yin Yang Direction. The Ox, Dragon Goat and Dog represent the element earth and are related to the third month of each season called between seasons, as you may see below.

Nr.	Animal	Year	Month Lunar	Yin Yang	Hour	Direct.	Element	Seasons	- Climat type & chi	
1	Rat	Zi	1 (Dic)	Yang	23 to 01	N	Water	Winter	**Winter** great Snow	Solstice
2	Ox	Chou	2 (Jan)	Yin	01 to 03	CENTER	Earth	Winter	Winter litlle cold	Cold Great
3	Tiger	Yin	3 (Feb)	Yang	03 to 05	E	Wood	between	Spring beguining	Rain Water
4	Rabbit	Mao	4 (Mar)	Yin	05 to 07	E	Wood	Spring	**Spring** insects	Equinox
5	Dragon	Chen	5 (Apr)	Yang	07 to 09	CENTER	Earth	Spring	Spring brightness	Rain Grain
6	Snake	Si	6 (May)	Yin	09 to 11	S	Fire	Between	Summer beguining	Grain full
7	Horse	Wu	7 (Jun)	Yang	11 to 13	S	Fire	Summer	**Summer** grains	Solstice
8	Goat	Wei	8 (Jul)	Yin	13 to 15	CENTER	Earth	Summer	Summer heat	Heat Great
9	Monkey	Shen	9 (Aug)	Yang	15 to 17	W	Metal	between	Autumn beguining	Heat Limit
10	Rooster	You	10 (Sep)	Yin	17 to 19	W	Metal	Autumn	**Autumn** white	Equinox
11	Dog	Xu	11 (Oct)	Yang	19 to 21	CENTER	Earth	Autumn	Autumn cold	Frost
12	Pig	Hai	12 (Nov)	Yin	21 to 23	N	Water	Between	Winter beguining	Slight Snow

Fig 30

The animal sign related to the year represent how others perceive you or how you present yourself. There are also animal signs or Branches, assigned by month, day, and hours of the day. The combination of one's birth year, month, day and hour are the 'Four Pillars' that determine your fate.

To sum it up, while a person might appear to be a Dragon because they were born in the year of the dragon, they might also be a Snake based on their birth month and an Ox based on their birthday and a Goat based on their birth hour.

Some basic characteristics of each animal year and personality, are described below, so you have a first basic idea of main traits of each one summing up this synthesis together with the natural animal type.

The number 1, is the Charming **RAT**, good in business and negotiation, checking details, namely on money and work issues, is ambitious and determined, this intellectual with a strong critical sense, can be extravagant and ambitious.

The serious **Ox**, stands for work, energy and resilience, balance and equilibrium, go together with patience, stubbornness, for this conventional and a little egocentric, submissive and passive but reliable friend, often unlucky in love.

The unpredictable **Tiger**, magnetic, captivating, full of vitality, is a courageous and selfish, but generous, loving authority and hating obeying personality that often rushes into things without proper consideration.

The diplomatic and tricky **Rabbit**, is a prudent, calm and discreet, deep and suspicious, intelligent, intuitive, hesitating but kind and generous, personality, devoted to sexual pleasures, with an instable and changing moods.

The mighty and egocentric **Dragon**, is and unpredictable, lucky being, virtuous, extravagant and original, so full of life that he can succeed in anything. This strong and inspiring fighter, knows its intelligence and follows its own advice. Intolerance and impulsivity can create some misjudgments.

Prudence, calculus, and wisdom, make the beautiful **Snake**, the hermetic and provident maquiavel, intuitive and tenacious, stable but mysterious, a good organizer. Stubborn, follows its own thinking, but is mostly liked and admired. Usually hard to copy with failure, is attracted to the occult side and can be quite jealous.

The intelligent but capricious **Horse**, mobile and adventurous, fast, persistent and popular, loves to be the central point and can easily lack of judgment in its brilliant, not always intelligent, way of optimizing all opportunities. Loves freedom and his major challenges is the impatience, the anxious and changeable moods.

The artistic, kind and sensitive **Sheep**, is a social and flexible, dreamer and moody, personality sensual but often with a disturbed love relationships. Loves harmony, but will fight under great provocations. Sometimes irresponsible, loves and searches for harmony.

The diplomatic, adaptable, clever and resourceful **Monkey**, is a pragmatic, and skilled, diplomat and competitor. Often egocentric, loves to laugh, only at others expenses, and is a little devious and unscrupulous, find always a way of jumping to another branch. Can easily fall in love but hard to find happiness.

The heroic and quixotic **Rooster**, as a profound sense of justice and is moral and honest. Loves to be the center of attentions, and is funny, altruistic and efficient, with a great intelligence and some doses of vanity, is strong willed and generous to friends. The weaker points are a deep anxiety and preoccupations.

The loyal **Dog**, constant, devoted and honest, is always watching, and faithful. Friendly, altruistic, logical and a bit pessimistic, can have its intuition often blind by suspicion, obstinate and pessimism, overestimating dangers. Defend its property fierce fully.

The epicurean and honest **Pig**, it's a pacific materialist goes straight to the point, can make good long term friendships. Often obstinate, is a peacemaker, giving away easily, decent and popular, has a nice humor and loves secrets.

To go deeper in this archetypes, we need to relate them with the respective element of the year they were born. For example a Goat usually an Earth related branch can be born under one of the other yearly four elements, making five different tonalities of the same personality.

The **Wood** element, can give to the Rat, a more quarrelsome tendency and enhance its deep fears, make the Ox more tenacious and fair, or the Tiger more tolerant and generous, as the Rabbit, and making a specially creative and happy Dragon, or a considerate and kind Snake, a disciplined Horse or a more practical and devoted Sheep, or even a careful and more ambitious Monkey and a kind and critical Rooster, with a more flexible and enchanting Dog, or a devious and subtle Pig.

The **Fire** element, would create an unpredictable Rat, more dynamic, an outspoken and difficult Ox, a transient and forceful Tiger, and a more emotional and secretive Rabbit, an explosive and dictatorial Dragon, with a more expressive and suspicious Snake, an more intelligent and excitable Horse, an active and outgoing Sheep, and a Reckless and Rash Monkey, an inflexible and enthusiastic Rooster, a Dog with more charisma and leadership, and a Pig more sensual and energetic.

The **Earth**, brings more stable and home loving Rats, loyal and sincere Ox's, persistent and objective tigers, Serious and materialistic Rabbits, Social and stable Dragons, likeable and practical Snakes, more calm and happy Horses, hardworking, sensitive, and self-reliable Sheep's, calm and honest Monkeys, analytical and compulsive Roosters, prudent and practical Horses, as well as friendly Pigs.

The **Metal** element, produces an emotional, materialist and jealous Rat, an artistic, arrogant and eloquent Ox, an extroverted optimistic Tiger, a devious and artistic Rabbit, a tougher, strong Dragon, a secretive and materialistic Snake, a friendly and egoistic Horse, an unstable but impenetrable Sheep, a combative and restless

Monkey, an industrious and committed Rooster, an inflexible and reassured Dog, and finally a more pushy and outgoing energetic Pig.

The **Water**, gives an intellectual and communicative Rat, a flexible but demanding Ox, a pleasant and realistic Tiger, a meditative and fragile Rabbit, a compromising and concentrated Dragon, an artistic and practical Snake, a funny and adaptable horse, a soft and weak passive Sheep, a secretive and sensitive monkey, an intellectual and obsessive Rooster, an easy going, wise Dog and a peaceful persuasive Pig.

Together with the 12 Earthly Branches (also called the 12 animals), we have the 10 Heavenly Stems that combine the 5 elements with their Yin Yang characteristics.

Characters represented by the Heavenly Stems and Earthly Branches allow us to derive in-depth insights into a person's character, potential, and destiny just by their mere appearance on a Ba Zi Chart.

Heavenly Stem	天干	tiān gān	Element	YIN-YANG
1	甲	jiǎ	Wood	Yang
2	乙	yǐ	Wood	Yin
3	丙	bǐng	Fire	Yang
4	丁	dīng	Fire	Yin
5	戊	wù	Earth	Yang
6	己	jǐ	Earth	Yin
7	庚	gēng	Metal	Yang
8	辛	xīn	Metal	Yin
9	壬	rén	Water	Yang
10	癸	guǐ	Water	Yin

Earthly Branch	地支	dì zhī	Hours	Animal	Hidden Element
1	子	zǐ	11pm-1am	Rat	Yang Water
2	丑	chǒu	1am-3am	Ox	Yin Earth
3	寅	yín	3am-5am	Tiger	Yang Wood
4	卯	mǎo	5am-7am	Rabbit	Yin Wood
5	辰	chén	7am-9am	Dragon	Yang Earth
6	巳	sì	9am-11am	Snake	Yin Fire
7	午	wǔ	11am-1pm	Horse	Yang Fire
8	未	wèi	1pm-3pm	Goat	Yin Earth
9	申	shēn	3pm-5pm	Monkey	Yang Metal
10	酉	yǒu	5pm-7pm	Rooster	Yin Metal
11	戌	xū	7pm-9pm	Dog	Yang Earth
12	亥	hài	9pm-11pm	Boar	Yin Water

Characteristics of the Heavenly Stems

Stem	甲 Jia	乙 Yi	丙 Bing	丁 Ding	戊 Wu	己 Ji	庚 Geng	辛 Xin	壬 Ren	癸 Gui
Meaning	Initiating Pushing Surging A sprout breaking through the earth.	Flexibility with strength. Early growth with bendable branches. Moving around barriers.	Expanding life force. All things are clear and obvious.	New life fully grown. Everything is at its strongest.	Blooming, flourishing. Luxuriant growth.	Distinguish-able features develop. Things start to become hidden inside.	Fullness, ripeness. Beginning of reversal.	Withdrawal Harvest.	Yang energy begins again inside/under water/earth.	Re-gathering the life force. Everything can be estimated.
Nr	First	Second	Third	Fourth	Fifth	Sixth	Seventh	Eighth	Ninth	Tenth
Element	Yang Wood	Yin Wood	Yang Fire	Yin Fire	Yang Earth	Yin Earth	Yang Metal	Yin Metal	Yang Water	Yin Water
Season	Spring		Summer		Four seasons		Autumn		Winter	
Organ	Liver		Heart		Spleen		Lungs		Kidneys	
Color	Green		Red		Yellow		White (Golden)		Black	
Flavor	Sour		Bitter		Sweet		Spicy		Salty	
Fruit	Plum		Apricot		Date		Peach		Chestnut	
System	Nervous System		Circulatory System		Digestive System		Respiratory		Excretory	
Body	Nerves		Blood		Muscles		Skin		Bones	
Direction	E		S		Center		W		N	
Animal	Green Dragon		Red Bird		Phoenix		White Tiger		Turtle	

Fig 31
Earthly Branches and Heavenly stems connections

Stems definition and the life cycle relations

The Stems are considered the most ancient system of time monitoring, since it translates the movement of Heavenly Chi into the agricultural rhythms of the seasons together with astronomy data from the planets movements.

Being a decimal system it was very similar to the Arabic numerals, so it was the most ancient time system totally objective without superstitious or feudal practices, as for instance the February, 1 1997, named as Year of Yi Chou, Month of Yi, day of Jia.

Between 1562 and 1066 BC, the Chinese Emperors and princes were named after these heavenly stems, like Da Ding (the Great Ding), Da Jia (the Great Jia), Wo Ding, Tian Yi, until King Zhou, that took the name of Emperor XIN.

From stem 1 to 10 the **Heavenly Stems** represent, the life cycle of people, things and situations, together with the human body parts, as follows in the charts below.

1. *Jia* –*Initiating, Pushing Surging. A sprout breaking through the earth*
2. **Yi** - *Flexibility with strength, early growth with bendable branches moving around barriers*
3. **Bing** - *Expanding life force. All things are clear and obvious*
4. **Ding** - *New life fully grown. Everything is at its strongest*
5. **Wu** - *Blooming Flourishing. Luxuriant growth*
6. *Ji* - *Distinguishable features develop. Things start to become hidden inside*
7. **Geng** - *Fullness Maturation Beginning of reversal*
8. **Xin** - *Withdrawal Harvest*
9. **Ren** - *Yang energy begins again inside/under earth/water*
10. **Gui** - *Re-gathering the life force. Everything can be estimated*

Life Cycle relations with Heavenly Stems   *recent years:*

1. Birth   1994,2004,2014
2. The nursing state of vulnerability   1995,2005,2015
3. The Childhood period of rapid growth   1996,2006,2016
4. The continuous growth of the youth times   1997,2007,2017
5. The prime years of physical development /   1998,2008,2018
    maturity
6. The peak performance of the middle age   1999,2009,2019
7. Aging takes place and weakness starts   2000,2010,2020
8. From weakness to the death   2001,2011,2021
9. Death and start of the new Chi to replace the old   2002,2012,2022
10. Dissipation of old Chi and emergence of new Chi   2003,2013,2023

Heavenly Stems and Human body relations

1. *Jia* - Spleen
2. **Yi** - Liver
3. **Bing** - Small Intestine
4. **Ding** - Heart
5. **Wu** - Ribs
6. **Ji** - Abdomen
7. **Geng** - Navel
8. **Xin** - Buttocks
9. **Ren** - Ankle
10. **Gui** - Leg

The dimensions of Time and Space, where also part of the Stems as they represent the four cardinal directions and the seasons.

STEM 1 and 2 represent Spring and East
STEM 3 and 4 represent Summer and South
STEM 5 and 6 represent End of summer and center
STEM 7 and 8 represent Autumn and West
STEM 9 and 10 represent Winter and North

Every earthly branch and its animal is associated to seasons and trigrams with all their interconnections. The reason why animals were named in connection with the seasons was probably to facilitate the peasants to remember the agricultural practices and labour associated with every agricultural cycle.

Besides the general characteristics of people based on the same Branch and Stem that we just provide here a summary of their main characteristics, you may later get more details from our web or the different sources available specific to this subject.

These personal profiles have some rules of compatibility among them that can be used to set up a non-conflicting supporting team with synergetic potential, at home, work, social or personal networks.

The 60 Years Cycle: *Earthly Branches and Heavenly stems*

The stems combine with the branches in a sequence shown below to form a cycle of 60 combinations known as the "60 Jia Zi".

This 60 Jia Zi is mapped to the year, month and day and repeated infinitely. For example the year 1924, 1984 and 2044 are all Jia (Stem) Zi (Branch) Year. The following years of 1925, 1985 and 2045 are all Yi (Stem) Chou (Branch) Year which is the next combination in the sequence.

The 60 Years Cycle and the Year Stem

1 to 10	11 to 20	21 to 30	31 to 40	41 to 50	51 to 60	Last Digit of the Year	Year STEM
JIA Rat	JIA Dog	JIA Monkey	JIA Horse	JIA Dragon	JIA Tiger	4	JIA
YI Ox	YI Pig	YI Rooster	YI Goat	YI Snake	YI Rabbit	5	YI
BING Tiger	BING Rat	BING Dog	BING Monkey	BING Horse	BING Dragon	6	BING
DING Rabbit	DING Ox	DING Pig	DING Rooster	DING Goat	DING Snake	7	DING
WU Dragon	WU Tiger	WU Rat	WU Dog	WU Monkey	WU Horse	8	WU
JI Snake	JI Rabbit	JI Ox	JI Pig	JI Rooster	JI Goat	9	JI
GENG Horse	GENG Dragon	GENG Tiger	GENG Rat	GENG Dog	GENG Monkey	0	GENG
XIN Goat	XIN Snake	XIN Rabbit	XIN Ox	XIN Pig	XIN Rooster	1	XIN
REN Monkey	REN Horse	REN Dragon	REN Tiger	REN Rat	REN Dog	2	REN
GUI Rooster	GUI Goat	GUI Snake	GUI Rabbit	GUI Ox	GUI Pig	3	GUI

Fig 32

Similarly if this month is Yi (Stem) Chou (Branch), then the next month is Bing (Stem) Yin (Branch) which is the next combination in the sequence. The same applies to the day, and to the hour: if today is Jia Zi then tomorrow is Yi Chou, and if this bi-hour is Ding You, the next bi-hour is Wu Xu the next combination in the cycle.

The cycle is repeated every 60 days. This is the base for every day in Chinese Solar (or Hsia) calendar being represented by four Jia Zi combinations namely the Stem and Branch of the year, month, day, and hour if present.

How to Calculate your Pillars of Destiny

The theory of the Four Pillars of Destiny is based on Yin Yang and the Elements (Wu Xing), and the pillars represent your Personality based on heavenly stems and earthly branches. They represent different aspects of your life as follows.

The Four **Pillars of Destiny** also called **Ba Zi or Eight Characters** is represented by four pairs of characters representing the year, month, day and hour of the birth date. Each pair is made up of two characters, one character from the Heavenly Stems (Element and Yin Yang), and one from the Earthly Branches (Animal and the element).

- **Year Pillar**: Family background and society.
- **Month Pillar:** Your early childhood and relationship with parents.
- **Day Pillar:** Your (DM) day master and relationship with partner/spouse.
- **Hour Pillar:** Relationship with children, your career and old age.

The Heavenly Stem of the Day pillar represents the the person self and is the most important Pillar. It is the reference point in the inter-relations with the other 7 elements in the charts of one's destiny.

The Earthly branch of the Day pillar is the marriage Pillar, and tells you the quality of your marriage.

The system will map out the 12 stages of your life cycle to reveal the strengths of the SELF-element within the framework

The excessive elements cause imbalance in your chart and are called unfavorable elements. The elements that you are lacking of, or those who produce the ones you need, are called your favorable elements or your lucky elements.

Within this Ba Zi system, the probability for two persons to have an identical heavenly luck is 1 in 12.96 million, and it would take 240 years to repeat another identical case within the next cycle.

The Year Pillar

Ten Heavenly Stems and Twelve Earthly branches as we presented above, combines and create a sexagenarian cycle. Next we present you a quick way to convert a year in western calendar into the one represented by stem and branch.

Heavenly Stem for the Year:

The last number of a year (first row) will indicate the year's Stem (number and name in second and third row):

4	5	6	7	8	9	0	1	2	3
1	2	3	4	5	6	7	8	9	10
Jia	Yi	Bing	Ding	Wu	Ji	Geng	Xin	Ren	Gui

Earthly Branch for the Year:

The reminder of the year divided by 12 will indicate the year's branch or that year animal. It will ranges between numbers "'0" and "11"

Rat	Ox	Tiger	Rabbit	Dragon	Snake	Horse	Goat	Monkey	Rooster	Dog	Pig
Zi	Chou	Yin	Mao	Chen	Si	Wu	Wei	Shen	You	Xu	Hai
4	5	6	7	8	9	10	11	0	1	2	3
Yang	Yin	Yang	Yin	Yang	Yin	Yang	Yin	Yang	Yin	Yang	Yin
Water	Earth	Wood	Wood	Earth	Fire	Fire	Earth	Metal	Metal	Earth	Water

Fig 33
Calculate your Earthly Branch for the year

Take the year 1993 for example. Last number 3 refers to Gui. 1993 divided by 12 equals an integer 166 with a reminder of 1. Number 1 refers to You or Rooster. So 1993 is *"Gui You"* or **Water Yin** and **Rooster** (Metal Yin) year.

The Month Pillar

The Month pillar has fixed early branches.

The lunar months are calculated from February on, and represent the Branches Yín, Mao, Chen, Si, Wu, Wei, Shen, You, Xu, Hai, Zi and Chou.

The heavenly stem is changing according to the year pillar. To calculate your Month Stem, please refer to the table below

Month Pillar of Destiny Earthly Branch

	Spring	Summer	Autumn	Winter
Month 1	Feb 4 to March 6	May 6 to June 6	August 8 to Sept. 8	Nov 7 to Dic 7
	Yang Wood Tiger	**Yin Fire Snake**	**Yang Metal Monkey**	**Yin Water Pig**
Month 2	March 6 to April 5	June 6 to July 7	Sept. 8 to Oct. 8	Dic 7 to Jan 6
	Yin Wood Rabbit	**Yang Fire Horse**	**Yin Metal Rooster**	**Yang Water Rat**
Month 3	April 5 to May 6	July 7 to August 8	Oct. 8 to Nov 7	Jan 6 to Feb 4
	Yang Earth Dragon	**Yin Earth Goat**	**Yang Earth dog**	**Yin Earth Ox**

EVALUATING the MONTH HEAVENLY STEM

	STEM of the YEAR	1 or 6	2 or 7	3 or 8	4 or 9	5 or 10
MONTH BRANCH						
1	*Tiger*	3	5	7	9	1
2	*Rabbit*	4	6	8	10	2
3	*Dragon*	5	7	9	1	3
4	*Snake*	6	8	10	2	4
5	*Horse*	7	9	1	3	5
6	*Goat*	8	10	2	4	6
7	*Monkey*	9	1	3	5	7
8	*Rooster*	10	2	4	6	8
9	*Dog*	1	3	5	7	9
10	*Pig*	2	4	6	8	10
11	*Rat*	3	5	7	9	1
12	*Ox*	4	6	8	10	2

Fig 34
Calculate your Month Pillar **Earthly Branch and Heavenly stem**

The Day Pillar
Formula to calculate the Heavenly Stem and Earthly Branch

The basic process is to know a day's stem and branch, so you should remember the stem and branch of the first day of that year in Chinese lunar calendar, that have different days in each month with 30 or 29 days.

One stem-branch cycle needs 60 days. If the stem and branch of the first day of that lunar month has been known, there is a way to extrapolate any day within the month, by the different extrapolation rules applied to bigger and lesser months.

You can use also the formula presented hereafter to calculate your day Pillar.

Consider:

X: Last two digits of the year
Y: The total days of that year in western calendar, up to and including the actual date itself. Be sure to evaluate correctly Leap years when February has 29 years
D: Division result
R: REMINDER, used to calculate energies and their phases
  • For the Stem if reminder is 0, then consider 10
  • For the Branch if the reminder is 0, then consider 12

FORMULA for 1901 to 2000 (including 2000)
You should always drop all fractions of numbers and use only the integer.

Always round up to the lower number.

$$\frac{5(X-1) + (X-1)/4 + 15 + Y}{60} = D$$

Example
1984 February 6
X= 84
Y= (31+6)= 37

Formula:
$\frac{5(84-1) + (84-1)/4 + 15 + 37}{60} = (415 + 20 + 15 + 37) / 60 = 487$
487 / 60 = 8 with a reminder of 7
D= 8
R = 7

Now lets calculate ;
STEM of the day: 7 / 10 = Reminder 7, so "GENG Stem"
BRANCH of the day: 7 / 12 = Reminder 7, so "Wu or Horse Branch"

FORMULA for 2001 to 2101 (including 2101)
You should always drop all fractions of numbers and use only the integer.

Always round up to the lower number.

$$\frac{5(X-1) + (X-1)/4 + Y}{60} = D$$

Example
2003 February 11
X= 3
Y= (31+11)= 42

Formula:
$$\frac{5(3-1) + (3-1)/4 + 42}{60} = \frac{(10 + 0 + 42)}{60} = \frac{52}{60}$$
52 / 60 = 0 with a reminder of 52
D= 0
R = 52

Now lets calculate ;
STEM of the day: 52 / 10 = Reminder 2, so "Yi Stem"
BRANCH of the day: 52 / 12 = Reminder 4, so "Mao or Rabbit Branch"

The Hour Pillar

Earthly Branch of the hour pillar is fixed, and starts with Zi (Rat) hour referring to 23:00-01:00, and so forth. For the Earthly Branches of 24 Hours (12 Shi Chen), please refer to the charts on Fig 31, and check the specific hour of each Animal or Branch.

To calculate the Heavenly Stem of each Hour, first calculate it's Branch as above, then using the Stem of the Day and the Branch of the Hour Pillars, please refer to Fig 35 to get the Hour Stem.

EVALUATING the HOUR HEAVENLY STEM

	STEM of the DAY	1 or 6	2 or 7	3 or 8	4 or 9	5 or 10
HOUR BRANCH						
1	*Rat*	1	3	5	7	9
2	*Ox*	2	4	6	8	10
3	*Tiger*	3	5	7	9	1
4	*Rabbit*	4	6	8	10	2
5	*Dragon*	5	7	9	1	3
6	*Snake*	6	8	10	2	4
7	*Horse*	7	9	1	3	5
8	*Goat*	8	10	2	4	6
9	*Monkey*	9	1	3	5	7
10	*Rooster*	10	2	4	6	8
11	*Dog*	1	3	5	7	9
12	*Pig*	2	4	6	8	10

Fig 35 Hour Stem

CASE STUDY on the Four Pillars of Destiny

The Four Pillars Chart for an individual born between 10 and 11 hours, February 11, 2003 in western calendar (lunar February 11, 2013).

Pillars	Hour	Day	Month	Year
Heavenly Stems	XIN	YI	JIA	GUI
Yin Yang & Element	*Yin Metal*	*Yin Wood*	*Yang Wood*	*Yin Water*
Earthly Branch	SNAKE	RABBIT	TIGER	GOAT
Yin Yang & Element	*Yin Fire*	*Yin Wood*	*Yang Wood*	*Yin Earth*

The year will represent its heritage, the month its upbringing, day and the hour the persons self and life.

The analysis show clearly an excess of Yin energy, needing to reinforce its YANG side, for example with several physical activity and colors. Also an excess of wood and a total lack of lack of Fire and short Metal, will need some adjustments, namely to fire which will control wood and at the same time producing earth that produces metal.

It has only eight characters, but the relation of the eight characters is very complex, according to the four pillars' representation theory meaning,

- **Year pillar** represents family background and society, parents and ancestors influence.
- **Month pillar** represents your early childhood and relationship with parents, brothers and sisters;
- **Day pillar** represents oneself, and relationship with partner/ spouse.
- **Hour pillar** represents offspring, relationship with children, your aura, career and old age.

To compensate any unbalance seen in a baby's Pillars, sometimes parents add this element in its name as an action to balance it. For instance you can compensate a character too Yin, by including Sun in the name of the child.

Old Chinese people believed that birth time is a kind of Chi or spirit, represented by an aura or energetic body, so people born in the Goat hour have an aura field of Goat. If the birth time is in Goat hour but closing to Monkey, the aura field has changed gradually to that of the Monkey hour.

7

Relationships and Human Environment

Heavenly Stems have their own characteristics which are connected to the relations between the Five Elements, besides the twelve animals or earthly branches relationships.

Among the ten heavenly stems, there are compatible and opposite relations, while among the Earthly Branches, there are more complex relationships combinations like, clash, and restriction or harm, as we will show you in our compatibility chapter hereafter.

Different relationships may have clear explanation regarding this Pillars interactions with the luck of one self and relatives.

We will present you now some basic rules to analyze and choose wisely your Human environment, to create a balanced and harmonious and enriching social network, and at the same time learn the lessons presented by the clashing characters that mirror in life your shadow side.

Earthly branch relations

The twelve animal signs can be divided into four groups of three. The groups are based on the assumption that each of the three animals concerned have similar ways of thinking or temperament, or at least the style of thinking and understanding.

These **golden triangles** represent the best combination of three signs, with common specific understanding.

Group One:
Rat, Dragon, Monkey
They are action oriented and show traits of intelligence. They can complement in intellect and are compatible with each other. Intense, restless, impetuous and enthusiastic group for bringing new ideas in the world, with potent positive and Yang energy.

Group Two:
Ox, Snake, Rooster
They are deep thinkers and always conscious about attaining their objectives. They are complementary to each other in intellect and habits. Best group for commerce and accumulation, rigid and communicative group with strong opinions with a strong business sense.

Group Three:
Tiger, Horse, Dog
They incline to freedom and have strong sense of personal ego. Idealistic and motivated, they excel in verbal communication and are mostly focus in relationships and social network. They can understand each other but sometimes are egoistical.

Group Four:
Rabbit, Sheep, Pig
They love peace and believe in mutual co-operation. They can be sympathetic and usually make great pair, based on feminine Yin energy. Peaceful and lucky group, focused on home and family, they are spiritual and harmony seekers.

We present you now the basic compatibility Chart between Animals or Earthly Branches.

Summary of the relationships between earthly branches

RAT
Good with: Rat, Dragon, Monkey
Moderate with: Ox, Tiger, Snake, Rooster, Dog, Pig
Difficult with: Rabbit, Horse, Sheep

OX
Good with: Rat, Rabbit, Monkey
Moderate with: Ox, Tiger, Snake, Rooster, Dog, Pig
Difficult with: Dragon, Horse, Sheep

TIGER
Good with: Dragon, Horse, Dog
Moderate with: Rat, Tiger, Sheep, Rooster, Pig
Difficult with: Rabbit, Monkey, Snake, Ox

RABBIT
Good with: Dragon, Sheep, Dog, Pig
Moderate with: Horse, Rabbit, Monkey, Snake, Ox
Difficult with: Rat, Tiger, Rooster

DRAGON
Good with: Rat, Rooster, Monkey
Moderate with: Sheep, Pig, Rabbit, Snake, Dragon, Horse
Difficult with: Tiger, Ox, Dog

SNAKE
Good with: Rooster, Ox Dragon, Horse, Dog
Moderate with: Rat, Sheep, Rabbit, Monkey,
Difficult with: Tiger, Snake, Pig

HORSE
Good with: Tiger, Sheep, Dog
Moderate with: Dragon, Rooster, Pig, Snake, Rabbit,
Difficult with: Rat, Horse, Monkey, Ox

SHEEP
Good with: Rabbit,, Horse, Pig
Moderate with: Monkey, Snake, Tiger, Sheep, Rooster, Dragon
Difficult with: Rat, Ox Dog

MONKEY
Good with: Rat, Dragon,
Moderate with: Sheep, Rooster, Pig, Rabbit, Monkey, Snake, Ox, Dog
Difficult with: Horse, Tiger

ROOSTER
Good with: Ox, Dragon, Snake
Moderate with: Rat, Sheep, Monkey, Pig, Horse, Tiger
Difficult with: Rooster, Rabbit, Dog

DOG
Good with: Horse, Tiger, Rabbit
Moderate with: Pig, Rat, Monkey, Snake, Ox, Dog
Difficult with: Dragon, Sheep, Rooster

PIG
Good with: Sheep, Rabbit
Moderate with: Tiger, Rooster, Pig, Ox, Rat,Dragon, Horse, Dog
Difficult with: Monkey, Snake

The next chart is a brief summary, synthetizing the level and type of bilateral compatibilities between these Branches, in a scale from 0 (the worse) to 10 (the best), combinations, as follows.

Value 10: Fantastic and most auspicious combination
Value 8: Excellent, harmonious and synergetic
Value 6: Good, and complementary
Value 4: Fair or just about reasonable combination
Value 2: Poor combination and probable clashes
Value 0: Severe clashes and conflicts, bad combination

Animal or Earthly Branches compatibility Chart

Earthly Branch	RAT	OX	TIGER	RABBIT	DRAGON	SNAKE	HORSE	GOAT	MONKEY	ROOSTER	DOG	PIG
RAT	8 well suited	10 happy steady	4 hot & cold	2 may argue	8 match suitable	2 couple volatile	2 poor match	1 poor match	9 very lively	4 need effort	4 lively couple	6 quite charm
OX		4 caring couple	5 couple unstable	5 couple unstable	4 tricky couple	8 mutual support	0 difficult match	2 steer clear	4 lively couple	8 good match	3 can be good	3 need effort
TIGER			2 happy steady	4 may be good	5 needs patience	0 Stear Clear	8 good ally	4 may workout	2 very rocky	6 hard work	8 strong ally	10 super match
RABBIT				8 loving couple	2 hard gooing	6 hard work	4 may workout	8 great fun	6 need effort	2 many conflicts	10 truly loving	8 super match
DRAGON					8 good match	4 may be good	6 lively couple	4 hot & cold	8 good match	10 wonder	2 not suitable	6 hard work
SNAKE						6 couple wonder	4 tricky couple	4 need effort	10 long lasting	8 couple wonder	6 quite charm	2 not match
HORSE							8 caring sharing	10 super match	4 quite hurtfull	6 may be good	8 good ally	5 up's & down's
GOAT								8 long lasting	6 may workout	4 hard work	2 tricky couple	8 mutual support
MONKEY									8 full of laughter	5 hard gooing	5 couple volatile	0 poles appart
ROOSTER										2 intense passion	0 poor match	4 needs effort
DOG											6 loyal loving	6 up's & down's
PIG												8 intense passion
ELEMENT	Water	Earth	Wood	Wood	Earth	Fire	Fire	Earth	Metal	Metal	Earth	Water
POLARITY	YANG	YIN	YANG	YIN	YANG	YIN	YANG	YIN	YANG	YIN	YANG	YIN

Fig36
Animal Branch Compatibility Chart

Feng Shui Your Mind

There are 3 groups of animals related to the star numbers of their year, creating some commonalities, as you can notice from the chart above, where we present some special cases.

- Rat, rabbit, horse and Rooster, can only fall in year's number: 1, 4 and 7
- Ox, Dragon, Sheep and Dog, can only fall in year's number: 3, 6 and 9
- Tiger, Snake, Monkey and Pig, can only fall in year's number: 2, 5 and 8

Groups of Branches together can help to balance a lack of energy in one Direction or one Element missing. For example, a lack of Fire element can be balanced with people of the chance set for Fire which are Tiger - Horse – Dog, as you can see in the next chart.

Special pairings of animals come together with a special type of energy, for business, long term relations, or other type of soul mates, but always with a strong bind together forming a Yin Yang pair with its next mate in the branch sequence:

Rat and Ox make the creativity and clever group, the Rat initiating what the Ox completes new creative projects.

The Tiger and the Rabbit, are the force and diplomacy, in growth and development.

The Dragon's magic and the Snake spirituality, combine harmoniously.

Horse and Goat combine Male and female energy in passion and sexuality.

The Monkey strategy and the Rooster activity, promote business and career improvement.

✦ 223 ✦

J.J. Lupi

The Dog and the Pig, create a domestic long life provided by the Dog and enjoyed by the Pig.

There are also **secret friends**, the helpers that support each other in life's most aspects,

Rat and Ox
Tiger and Pig
Rabbit and Dog
Dragon and Rooster
Horse and Goat
Snake and Monkey

Harmony & Prosperity			
Water	Metal	Fire	Wood
Monkey	Snake	Tiger	Pig
Rat	Rooster	Horse	Rabbit
Dragon	Ox	Dog	Goat

DIRECTIONS Peaks of Energy			
East	South	West	North
Tiger	Snake	Monkey	Pig
Rabbit	Horse	Rooster	Rat
Dragon	Goat	Dog	Ox

BILATERAL COMBINATIONS

+ Good With:		Element		- Bad With:	
Rat	Ox	Earth		Rat	Horse
Tiger	Pig	Wood		Ox	Sheep
Rabbit	Dog	Fire		Tiger	Monkey
Dragon	Rooster	Metal		Rabbit	Rooster
Snake	Monkey	Water		Dragon	Dog
Horse	Goat	Fire		Snake	Pig

Fig37
Animal Branch Compatibility

Finally the **Crosses** or opposites getting together, are present when you have in your pillars chart two pairs of opposite Branches. These opposites, if they are ALL four present in your chart can be very auspicious in some way. Beware if there are any of the four opposites missing because then you may have some problems.

Three Crosses are possible:

Fame, Love and Power, where the four opposites became cooperative for very active and hot for love and money. They represent balance through tension and comprises the Branches of Rat, Horse, Rabbit and Rooster.

Artistic, Cultural and Literary capabilities are present if you have Ox, Goat, Dragon, and Dog Branches altogether.

Travel, Change and Movement are the motto for the Tiger, Monkey, Snake and Pig, when together it's an exhausting combination in permanent questioning, and they can be moving towards or away from, so looking for something or escaping from something.

Eartlhy Branches generates sets of and the three combinations to form each one of the **five elements**:

Monkey, Rat, Dragon combine and form Water,
Pig, Rabbit, Goat combine and form Wood,
Tiger, Horse, Dog combine and form Fire.
Rooster, Ox combine and form Metal,
Dragon, Dog, Ox, Goat combine and forms Earth.

The opposition between branches runs from strong to week harms:

1- Six Clashes of the opposing Earthly Branches:
Zi vs Wu, Yin vs Shen, Mao vs You, Chen vs Xu, Si vs Hai, Chou vs Wei

2- Punishment of Earthly Branches:
   Special - Yin vs Si, Si vs Shen, Shen vs Yin
   Ungrateful – Chou vs Xu, Xu vs Wei, Wei vs Chou
   Rudeness – Zi vs Mao
   Self Punishment – Chen vs Chen, Wu vs Wu, You vs You, Hai vs Hai
   Earthly Branches Harm:
   Zi vs Wei, Chou vs Wu, Yin vs Si, Mao vs Chen, Shen vs Hai,
   You vs Hai

Heavenly Stems relations

Their compatibility matrix, presents with the rules explained below.

Heavenly Stems and the Five Compatibilities are based on the elements, as in the following example: Wood is the corresponding element in Wu Xing to Jia, so is Earth to Ji. Wood grows in earth, so they are compatible combination.

So the compatibilities are:

   Jia and Ji,
   Yi and Geng,
   Bing and Xin,
   Ding and Ren,
   Wu and Gui

Personal Element define peoples type of relations

The interaction of the Element characteristics of each person predispose a certain type of relationships, as we can see in the next figure relating to a Women Metal and a Man Earth.

Case for Woman Metal and Man Earth

If you are:		This element relates to you as :				
		Wood	Fire	Earth	Metal	Water
Woman						
Metal		Father	Husband	Mother	Siblings	Children
Life Aspects		Wealth Money	Status Presure Power	Resource Support Authority	Coleagues Competition	Inteligence Expressive Ability
Man						
Earth		Children	Mother	Siblings	-	Wife Father
Life Aspects		Status Presure Power	Resource Support Authority	Coleagues Competition	Inteligence Expressive Ability	Wealth Money

Fig38

8

Chi Numbers in the Magic Square

Based on the Ba Gua matrix, where we put the numbers of our birth date, we may check the main energy present or missing in our life chart.

There are special energies represented by each row, either Vertical or Horizontal in the Ba Gua structure, so the CHI Numbers associated with each mansion and row, present specific Characteristics related with the different lines, as follows.

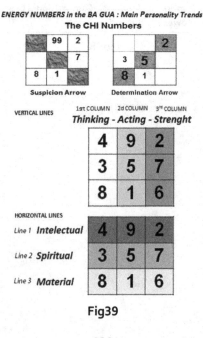

Fig39

Through the analysis of the numbers you can sense the type and level of basic energy of the individual, after putting the birth date numbers in their corresponding cases of the Magic Square.

A complete set of numbers in one full line, either vertical, horizontal or transversal, create an *Arrow.*

There may be **Strength Arrows**, if all numbers are present in the arrow, or **Weakness Arrows**, if all numbers are missing in the arrow, so we will have some common characteristics of the person character, according to the set of arrows present in their Map.

Missing Numbers and name of the Weakness Arrows,

Frustration, missing numbers 8, 5 and 2
Suspicion, missing numbers 4, 5 and 6
Emotional autism, missing numbers 3, 5 and 7
Procrastination, missing numbers 6, 7 and 2
Confusion, missing numbers 8, 3 and 4
Failure, missing numbers 8, 1 and 6
Bad Memory, missing numbers 4, 9 and 2
Self-doubt, missing numbers 1, 5 and 9

And the full lines, as Strenght arrows, in another hand, presented as follows,

Line Numbers and the Strength Arrows,

Determination, with arrow numbers 8, 5 and 2
Emotional balance, with arrow numbers 4, 5 and 6
Spirituality, with arrow numbers 3, 5 and 7
Intellect, with arrow numbers 4, 9 and 2
Litigation, with arrow numbers 1, 5 and 9
Prosperity, with arrow numbers 8, 1 and 6
Politician, with arrow numbers 4, 3 and 8
Energetic action, with arrow numbers 2, 7 and 6

J.J. Lupi

Case Study *(from the figure above)*

Let's suppose you were born the February 8, 1979, at 12.00h in Luxembourg. Your Chi numbers are showed in first figure above (8/2/1979): one 1, one 2, one 7, one 8 and two 9, and after they are correctly placed over the magic square, we may observe the presence or absence of several energies.

The most important feature of this case configuration is the missing sequence in the line corresponding to numbers 4, 5, 6. This is called an empty ARROW and in this case is associated with a **suspicious character**, as all the special configurations are associated with special traits of personality.

Also we can have a **Strenght** ARROW **full** line with all numbers present, as in the case of the second figure above, for someone born in May 5, 2013, in this case it will be called a **"determination"** arrow associated with this trait of personality.

9

Life cycles and periods of crisis

Actually, there is a large list of personal development and healing systems, based on human profiling and life cycles, like the Eneagram or the Time Line Therapy in Neuro Linguistic Programing (NLP).

The Feng Shui, also provide us one of the most ancient proved and studied framework on this domains: 9 different basic types of human nature and faith, influenced through time, in harmony with heaven and earth energetic cycles, with the stars and nature.

The full information about each individual person, things or situations is based on nine energy qualities, interacting with the 5 elements and the Yin and Yang forces. All these are integrated within the GUA number of each individual.

The Ba Gua of the Later Heaven is the one used for this earthly calculation, as it deals with the impact of heaven energies in contact with nature. In this case we will retain for calculations, the Yang or Masculine GUA number of the Year.

This analysis is developed under what is called the "Flying Stars" school of Feng Shui. According to the energies from the nine Trigrams, combining Heaven and Earth energies mediated by Humans and representing these tree different levels, with the interplay of the Yin / Yang Balance, on a complex system of Heavenly stems and earthly branches, within cycles of 9, 20 and 64 years.

To allow us to have some guidance and references of our specific basic nature and for the purpose of this first approach, we are going to present a simplified system to access the basic energies and the life cycles involved.

This classification is based on the Star of the Year, moving through the path of the Flying Stars and across the nine Mansions of the LO SHU, we saw in the first chapter.

The Flying Stars and human profiles

The 9 Flying Stars present the general context framing your life, whether the 10 years stem cycle, concerns mainly our mental and vibrational, and the 12 years branches return, has major influence over our external appearance and material achievements.

The Flying Stars Chi, are the different energies repeated in a cycle of 9 years, 9 months, and 9 days, that combining the different energetic levels of the 5 elements of nature: fire 9, as the peak energy and water 1, as the lowest energetic level, mediated by number 5 or yellow earth, the most balanced of the stars. Stars 3 and 4 wood, representing an energetic level of springtime above 6 and 7, the metal stars of autumn.

After finding the Number representing your Star or the Gua (Yang) of your birth year, you can already identify the main characteristics of your first Pillar of Destiny, in the short profiles I present you below.

Regarding the 9 years cycle of the Flying Stars, the central number used for the LO SHU or magic square, is the Masculine or Yang Gua. Here we do not separate a feminine Gua that differs from the masculine numbers, as we do to define our best directions as seen previously.

You can find your star for the year and each month in the matrix below.

Profiles of Individuals born under a specific Star, can be found below, followed by an analysis of the main energies they will face, when passing through the nine years cycle of each Star dominant energy.

Flying Star number for the Year (1900 -2059)

DECADE	0	1	2	3	4	5	6	7	8	9
YEARS										
1900	1	9	8	7	6	5	4	3	2	1
1910	9	8	7	6	5	4	3	2	1	9
1920	8	7	6	5	4	3	2	1	9	8
1930	7	6	5	4	3	2	1	9	8	7
1940	6	5	4	3	2	1	9	8	7	6
1950	5	4	3	2	1	9	8	7	6	5
1960	4	3	2	1	9	8	7	6	5	4
1970	3	2	1	9	8	7	6	5	4	3
1980	2	1	9	8	7	6	5	4	3	2
1990	1	9	8	7	6	5	4	3	2	1
2000	9	8	7	6	5	4	3	2	1	9
2010	8	7	6	5	4	3	2	1	9	8
2020	7	6	5	4	3	2	1	9	8	7
2030	6	5	4	3	2	1	9	8	7	6
2040	5	4	3	2	1	9	8	7	6	5
2050	4	3	2	1	9	8	7	6	5	4

Chinese Lunar Months	Basic	Yearly	Star
	1, 4, 7	5, 2, 8	3, 6, 9
February 4 – March 5	8	2	5
March 6 – April 5	7	1	4
April 6 – May 5	6	9	3
May 6 – June 5	5	8	2
June 6 – July 7	4	7	1
July 8 – August 7	3	6	9
August 8 – September 7	2	5	8
September 8 – October 8	1	4	7
October 8 – November 7	9	3	6
November 8 – Dicember 7	8	2	5
Dicember 8 – January 5	7	1	4
January 6 – February 3	6	9	3

Fig40
Calculate your Star for the year and the month

STAR 1 – Water Star of the North – trigram KAN

Black

Flexible like water, sometimes a little too much, they can be deep and active, or turbulent and agitated as a lake or a river or a cascade. Free spirits, they care about their personal space, are sentimental creative, artistic and philosophers. These personalities are quite adaptable and an easy follower, that should cultivate happiness and optimism, paying special attention to their human environment because of its strong influence over their life's. Great mediators, after a usually difficult family childhood, its best period will be around 40's where they should take some resources for older times.

Very sensible to their relations, they have stable relationships, with a passionate and sexual focus.

The body liquids, and their organs, also bones and nerves, should be payed special attention.

STAR 2 – Earth Star of SW – trigram KUN

Black Earth

A multitude of relations for service and cooperation, this star represent the late summer period for harvest. Gentle, loyal and sociable, they like to help and create very good and supportive relations with others, so they should always look for cooperative activities instead of lonely ones. When in doubt they may lack punch. Their best years are from 45 to 47.

Communication flows in relationships, with a special sensibility to the other needs, sometimes with excessive care for details, there is a risk of suffocate the other, in routines, protectionism and free expression of emotions.

Usually heavy bodies they need to watch they digestive system, tongue, throat and skin.

STAR 3 – Wood Star of E – Trigram CHEN

Green Jade of Wood

Spring and renewal, independent spirits by themselves or forced by circumstances, they easily attract enemies from their aggressive behavior and lack of concern for others. Ambitious, they will lead a life of up and downs, always catching the next wave of opportunities, making friends that admire their optimistic character. Often they tend to let unfinished projects, or let them to others. Take your time, evaluate all possibilities, and don't rush for your goals. Best years usually are between 34 and 38.

Impulsivity also shapes their relationships, since early ages, that often do not last long, because they tend to create illusions mostly based on external appearances, and don't cope well with routine, being prone to jealousy and anger.

Liver, gall bladder and depressive moods are their main health issues, for these sportive natures. Attention to phobias due to their extreme reactivity.

STAR 4 – Wood Star of SE – Trigram SUN

Green Wood

Wind, dispersion and penetration, these individualist fluctuating sensible and practical characters, have great capacity to generate wealth. Often lacking of strong will, they can be easily controlled by others, changing opinions on others arguments, they can present between sensible, trustable, and stable, to chaotic and destructive behaviors, sometimes making them change residency. Attached to structures and social conventions, although they are usually good counselors, they lack trust in themselves, questioning and hesitating often. They profit for showing themselves has they are, develop their character, and trust their very developed intuition, and beware also of flattery. They should find balance their before 38, after will be more difficult.

Very seductive they need to beware of getting into relationships for material or social interest. They lack of understanding their romantic partners, leading them to errors and unsatisfying behaviors. They may have difficulties in finding love happiness due to their dreams and idealism.

Watch out your nerves and your liver. Digestion, genitals and respiratory system to be taken care specially. Best vitality after meals.

STAR 5 – Earth Central Star

Yellow Earth

This base central star connects to earth trigrams Ken (masculine mountain), and Kun (feminine earth), two main forces that support them.

The beginning and the end of a cycle, this charismatic leaders, are ambitious and extreme personalities with a high self-esteem that can range from openness and generosity, to rigidity and stupidity, but always looking either moral or confusing. They will have either a complete success at material, emotional and spiritual level, or suffer reverses of life, due to the unpredictable events of their time line. They should not rush, take their time, and reconsider themselves once in a while.

Passionate natures, they need to feel loved, and sometimes even look for multiple partners, in their search for love.

Their blood pressure, stomach and spleen should be watched, namely in humid and hot regions of the globe. Chronic fatigue is also to watch out for these resistant persons.

STAR 6 – Metal Star of NW – Trigram CHIEN

White metal

The wise leader, idealistic, ambitious, paternalists and auto critical, they tend to be active, persevering and constant. All the leadership qualities are found in these personalities auto sufficient, with high ideals with sometimes lack of modesty. Conflicts result mostly from attached egoistic attitudes, opposing them to others because of their horror to lose. They overcome all difficulties, with a huge capacity and efficient organization. To direct and sharp they risk to offend others easily, so don't feel very comfortable in social events.

Materialistic by nature they are also spiritual and charitable individuals, even if their close relations and subordinates, have hard times with them. Family and loyalty are key important in their values. Often over demanding on themselves and others. Their best period is usually after 40.

Dominating, excessive yang is the main factor affecting their relations, so these personalities should reinforce and open to their Yin complementary qualities. Family values are at most important, and they may appear insensitive and cold towards feelings. Very sensible to opposite sex charms, under a calm and controlled appearance.

Some headaches, heart, skin and respiratory problems, are common issues together with inflammatory processes.

STAR 7 – metal Star of W – Trigram TUI

Red metal

A deep desire for freedom, willing to fully enjoy life pleasures, this joyful, optimistic and sweet natured personalities, have very good diplomatic skills, are usually excellent public speakers, but better talkers then listeners, and often don't care much about hierarchies. Material security is very important for them, and they are very good at evaluating situations, using their great intuitive powers, allowing them to easily anticipate situations.

Looking younger and very persuasive persons they are often admired and able to influence and be followed by others. Sensual and eccentric personalities, they have a great need to please others, and can hardly say no. Several relations are common, and lots of seduction before marriage, or they may even keep themselves single, with their desire for freedom.

Their best years usually com after 40's, they need to be more persistent in their projects and to be more cooperative with others, even if they need to give up some of their freedom, in order to get more help. Avoid excess intellectual melancholy.

Their head and bones, together with their nervous system skin and intestines, are the main health concerns. During their youth, they often lack of regularity in their meals and leisure, causing digestive problems later.

STAR 8 – Earth Star of NE – Trigram KEN

Withe earth

Strong willed and presenting a spiritual force like the mountain, these personalities, tend to be rigid and resistant to change. They may appear cold and distant sometimes and it can be difficult to communicate with and get into their personal world or cooperate with them.

Full of energy, they work out slowly but steady and secure building their way to create and accumulate abundance in their lives. Sweet nature and soft, they are honest and may lead others to follow their views.

Often childish and jealous, they tend to be conservative and creative at the same time. They learn usually through the school of life, and behave quite unconventionally. Trustful and conventional partners in relationships, they are persistent to get their sentimental objectives but they also disregard and are quite rude to those lacking to give them enough attention.

Most of the times a little rigid personalities, practicing regular physical activity would balance their psycho-physiological health, and watch specially their bones, intestinal and respiratory systems.

STAR 9 – Fire Star of S – Trigram LI

Purple fire

Charismatic and joyful character, impulsive, sensible with emotional fluctuations, they may tend to extinguish their fire under depressive moods. Passionate and enthusiastic they have a natural leadership qualities at high level, and attract people, followers and friends easily, from their Intelligent and witty personalities, communicative, generous, and benevolent qualities, although they present often a superiority look. They need mostly, constancy, perseveration and patience.

These magnetic personalities can lose motivation and become voluble when out of balance. Considering appearances important, with artistic qualities besides a materialistic look, they will spend lots of energy to achieve a nice and beautiful status in life, with a very easy critical mind, and an horror to lose. Often spending too much energy on the fist half of life they can notice it in the second half, they should rely more in themselves then on others. Meditation and compassion, can balance the fear of failure with associated anger.

Their romantic and loving personalities understand easily their mates, but can conflict with their love for freedom, and the fantasies they dream about relationships, although they can be trustful partners while the relation is harmonious, they have great difficulty in keeping secrets, and they get bored easily. Their seductive power through the look and the voice attract easily partners but there are too possessive which creates often difficulties in the relation.

Usually tall above average this persons are extremely energetic with penetrating eyes, may have problems mostly in heart rhythms, eyes, insomnia.

Star of the Month

The Life cycles energies and transition periods within the flying stars path.

Energy moves! As we have seen before, in the chapter on impermanence, the universe is in motion, you are happy and then you are sad, the cold winter follows a hot summertime, the economic cycles of expansion follow the regression periods and major crises.

The structures where we live are the stable energies (meaning that they wil move on slowly long cycles), that surround us and frame the shorter and the unpredictable changes on the balance Yin / Yang and specific energies balance.

There are stable trends, and there are more fluctuating ones, like during the year the seasons follow each other in a non-changeable sequence, but within each season you can find a rainy day in summer and a sunny day in winter, like in a life time, birth, growth, aging and dead, follows an inevitable path, but within each cycle you can find ups and downs, health and illness.

You cannot seat on the top and expect to stay there all your life. Because things never stay the same, we better move with it!

To help us to take advantage of positive phases and counteract the negative ones, the Feng Shui School of the Flying Stars, has developed the concept of the Four Pillars of Destiny that frame our life cycles, and show us our basic energy.

These are based on our own date of birth, regarding the Trigram (Gua) for the year, the month, the hour, together, with our earthly branch (or animal zodiac).

For all these calculations the Chinese Lunar calendar is used, based upon the traditional calendar over the rhythm of life, more depending on the moon cycles, instead of our Gregorian actual artificial one.

In this Chinese calendar the new year starts around the 4 of February, used in most common evaluations, but it varies between the 21 January and the 21 February, so pay attention to your calculation if you want an exact figure.

The 9 years cycle and the Lucky Stars

To make your yearly and monthly energy previsions, you need to locate your Birth Star, into the Lo Shu Square of the year in reference,

✓ First calculate your star number.
✓ Select the Lo Shu with the number in the center, corresponding to the number of the year you are looking for the assessment.
✓ Next, take note of the mansion where your star is in this year Lo Shu.
✓ Then you check in the Standard Lo SHU what the base number star of that mansion is. These number energies will be the ones you will face in that year.

For example:

One person woman born the 9 May 1993, at 1330h,

✓ Her birth Star number 7.

To evaluate her year 2014, which is year star number 4,

✓ First we look for the Lo Shu with central mansion number 4
✓ Her Birth star 7 is located, in the Mansion corresponding to number 8 in the standard LO SHU square.

Star number 8 will be running her year 2014!

The 9 years cycle and the Lucky Stars

The LO SHU and the 9 Years cycle

9	5	7
8	1	3
4	6	2

1	6	8
9	2	4
5	7	3

2	7	9
1	3	5
6	8	4

3	8	1
2	4	6
7	9	5

4	9	2
3	5	7
8	1	6

5	1	3
4	6	8
9	2	7

6	2	4
5	7	9
1	3	8

7	3	5
6	8	1
2	4	9

8	4	6
7	9	2
3	5	1

Fig41
Flying Stars Matrix

Water Mansion 1

It is hard to expand in winter time, so no action is favored, but instead a time for preparing, structure and organize. The deep inner secrets personal and illicit may be revealed. Beware of everything related with liquids, water, alcohol, and others.

You may feel isolated, and excluded from others, hidden below the water, so it is the time to explore our inner issues, cultivate the spirit, and meditate on future actions. Control yourself and accumulate strength for the next step.

This is the winter season, where you need to make your analysis, reflections, plans, and beware of unpredictable health and financial problems that may arrive. Only new beginnings of studies are favored together with all sorts of introspections. Elements and stars in conflict related to numbers (earth) 2, 5, 8 and (fire) 9.

Earth Yin Mansion 2 -

This is the recollection phase. Now is the moment to materialize what was planned in Mansion 1. Set up and go, letting new plans, creativity, social and economic developments, for the moment and give birth to what was planned. Avoid anxiety and negativity that may arise.

Learn how to accept life routine and enjoy it, without wishing to lead it. Avoid eating to much and take note and manage of your emotional states, without putting yourself in the front line. Elements and stars in conflict related to numbers (water) 1, and (wood) 3,4, are more prone to changes then other stars.

Wood Yin, Thunder Mansion 3

The Thunder announces the explosive expansion, progress and growth, full of opportunities. The rapid flow of this energy demands quick decisions, but serious commitment, and wise evaluation of goals, because it will run for a fast success, but also failure if not seriously taken. Beware of jealousy of others achievements.

Exploring all options and plans analyzed in mansion 2, travelling, and keeping an open mind on all lucky chances that may appear, may end up, in a favorable changes.

Spring time and creativity together will need a little rest, personal care and life balance to avoid overworking and stress, and excess of joy and anger, and their counterparts of sadness and melancholy. Elements and stars in conflict related to numbers (earth) 2, 5, 8 and (metal) 6, 7. Best advice is to count to three before taken options.

Wood Yang, Wind Mansion 4

The winds of the intelligence can penetrate and get everything with concentration, speed and open mind, achieving fast growth and maturity, experience and pragmatic achievements. Results from previous year multiply and you access easy material rewards, respect and trust from others.

Keep yourself on the trail of your previous plans and avoid entering in new unknown areas. Just control your impulsivity, and secure your basic structure, because it will be your support for growth. Keep your promises within your limits, because winds may change.

Within a very pragmatic and materialistic year you will find pleasant occasions for leisure and travel, getting around with friends, and socializing in nice environments, with an easy flow of communication and understanding.

Reinforce your immunity and nervous system, liver and lungs. Elements and stars in conflict related to numbers (earth) 2,5,8 and (metal) 6, 7.

Earth, Central Mansion 5

Every nine years you will be back in this mansion, your birth place, restarting a new cycle. All opportunities may arrive in an unpredictable way, so you should be focused and centered to take the best chances. Choose wisely and act carefully. You will find spiritual fulfillment and its recommended that you control pride and egocentric behaviors.

The results of the full period will show up here, and the starting period for long term action plans. Also it may be the beginning or the ending period for soul mates or strong relationships.

Very demanding and fluctuating period, full of requests of your attention from others, be altruistic. It is also the moment where you should finish what you have started, to close the cycle.

There is a possibility of psychosomatic heart and digestive issues, and risk of small tumors or cysts. Elements and stars in conflict related to numbers (water) 1 and (wood) 3,4.

Metal Yang, Mansion 6

This is the moment to recollect the fruits, abundance and satisfaction from past efforts. You already know your skills, and capacity, that are also recognized by others, so you may proceed to engage in further and higher targets. These will demand intellectual and concentration efforts to cope with your huge targets that will keep you pretty busy, and you better focus on clear targets for your ambitions, as the way of the superior man.

Your leadership should avoid pride and arrogance, to not create enemies, even though you will be admired and full of self-confidence, with feelings of unlimited power.

Health issues from the head, circulation and pressure, upper respiratory system, together with skin and sun exposure, and neurosis, should be prevented as well as driving problems and sudden stops.

Elements and stars in conflict related to numbers Water 1, Fire 9 and Wood 3.

Metal Yin Lake, Mansion 7

This is the relaxing period of joy and celebration, after recollection, a brief moment of feelings of material security and fulfillment after the work done, more than spiritual satisfaction. You can now rest, travel for leisure and relax, develop your social network, although this will use part of your gains and savings, you may have lucky unexpected sources of funding.

Use this time to develop energetic practices to enhance your spiritual development. Contacts, social and potential opportunities may not lead to any achievements, so don't spend too much energy on those, and avoid misunderstood.

Watch out your mouse and respiratory system. The elements and stars in conflict related to numbers (fire) 9 and (wood) 3, 4.

Mountain Earth Yang Mansion 8

Like the hermit retiring to the mountain, this is a good period to withdraw from the scene and find your inner deep self, and connect to your spiritual being. External issues may impact the result of your decisions and you may need to change them, so take your time before deciding and be flexible on your decisions. Avoid starting associations during this period.

During this vulnerable time even if you feel needy, insecure and full of internal conflicts, keep yourself flexible and avoid conflicts. A major emotional and spiritual development can start now give place to deep structural changes.

Avoid fights, and be cautious with legal issues. During this period of easy misunderstood, be very clear and get some feedback to be sure of what was understood from what you say, and favor your own evaluations.

Major life changes may be favored during this time, if you give enough time and reflection on them, accepting to retire and study all aspects, because it is a good moment to start.

Pay attention to others actions to not harm you, and take care of your physical body specially your blood circulation.

Elements and stars in conflict related to numbers (wood) 3, 4 and (water) 1, so accept to give yourself some more time, and avoid changes during this period, even if you feel like it.

Fire Mansion 9

This year of manifestation, expansion and expression, allows you to manifest yourself fully. Very socially active period will bring you recognition and visibility to all capacity, your ambitions, projects, together with the positive and negative aspects of your life and intentions.

Artistic gifts should be developed, and you may try different lifestyles, and unknown territories, together with cultivating a more openness within your relations and expect the same in return.

All your realizations will come to light and you may change of residence, friends, relationships and even your image. Create solid bases now, for your projects. Avoid the shadows of pride and superficiality; you may encounter problems with old friends.

Written documents from the past can be lost or bring some problems, as can do also any type of scandals during this phase, and your health should balance excess yang Joy and Yin depression, and prevent your heart, eyes and circulation issues.

Elements and stars in conflict related to numbers (metal) 6, 7 and (water) 1, watch out for circulatory problems and you may feel some discomfort with all this fire phase.

Lo Shu Life Cycle
Number, Natural Phenomena and Concept

4 Wind	9 Fire	2 Earth
Power Abundance	Fame Spiritual alignement Image Projection	Partners Relationships Associates
Fast Growth	*Self-Knowledge*	*Germination*
3 Thunder	5 Tai Chi	7 Lake
Bases (Origins) Nuclear Family Psycho Genealogy	Health Main Energy	Criativity Children
Growth Begin	*End and Begining*	*Celebrate*
8 Mountain	1 Water	6 Heaven
Knowledge Spirituality	Career Life Projects Goals	Mentors, Friends Helpers, Journeys Traveling
Stillness	*Planning*	*Prosperity*

Chinese Daily Calendar

Ancient drawings of the 5 elements and relations

Fig 42
the 9 years life cycle

10

Managing Time and Space

Time and **space** are **heaven** and **earth,** and the human condition is to be in interplay between both. This means that optimizing and aligning our life with both will provide us the best chances for a successful and happy life.

Regarding **Time** one of the most effective and simple ways to take the best from time management is to follow the Flying stars periods for the year, month, day and even the hour, for the most important and accurate events, as we showed you above.

Regarding **Space,** besides what you learned from first part of this book, there is an important issue that is Movement. In what directions you move or travel when doing business or optimizing your social or love life?

There are two main ways to take into account direction of movement: the geographic, and the Lo Shu approaches.

The geographical approach, is based on the rotation movement of earth and the flow of energy it generates. The planet Earth rotation movement is from east to west, which as too main consequences in what concerns us:

- The speed of things in the earth surface in the North and South poles is much less then it is in the equatorial circle.

This means that the dispersion effect will be higher as we move south in the north hemisphere (moving to the equator), and the opposite in the south hemisphere (high dispersion as we move north to the equator).

- The easiest flow from east to west, aligned together with the direction of the earth rotation movement.

This means that it will always be easier to go from east to west than the opposite, as many frequent flyers have experienced already when coming home from west to east, with higher difficulty recovering from jet leg, then when they fly East-West.

This are some of the main reasons why most of conquests where made from North to South and from East to West, and the well-known difficulties of Hitler, Napoleon and even Alexander the Great, essays to conquer Russia and eastern countries always failed and always presented great difficulties.

The Lo Shu approach, is based on centuries of observation of the main energies Yin Yang and heaven energies arriving to the earth, and finally arrved to the conclusion that there were four main directions to avoid to move towards, based on the Lo Shu Square of the year, month, day and hour.

These directions are:

- going towards and away to the *absolute actual direction* of the location of number 5 (N, S, E, W, NE, NW, SE, SW),
- going towards your personal number or lucky star, and they present each one the following dangers:
  - Towards number 5 is the worst direction, with Yang aspects with different problems during traveling, health issues and obstacles to achieve financial and other proposed goals.

○ Away from number 5, is the Yin shadow side of the difficulties with unexpected and negative subtle influences.

○ Towards and away from the actual location of your personal number is also to avoid. If this number is in the center (as the number 5 in the basic Lo Shu), you should avoid at all traveling because it is a period where you should be quiet and profit for inner wisdom development and personal growth, preparing the growth in the following years.

The main issues are based on biological influences, so you can try to optimize your travel dates and if you really need to do it then organize your travel with different directions within one or two weeks in order to counterbalance this influences, or travel with a colleague that do not share the negative directions and let him take decisions, and also you can start adapting your life and eating style to the culture of your destiny.

11

How to do Personal Feng Shui

The Personal Feng Shui, concerns Heavenly information, namely predetermination and timing issues, and allow you to check whether you are consistently connected and centered with your life mission and spiritual path.

The challenge here is how to accept and integrate these different predetermined aspects, that will allow you to live a coherent and fulfilled happy life.

A perfect time management, understanding impermanence, life cycles and the energy of each period will let you choose wisely whether to act or hold back in the right moment to avoid stress and waste energy, so to have the best "useful attitude" in every moment of your life.

You can use the formulas presented in this chapter in order to identify your main life issues from strategic issues; to the main balance of elements and Yin Yang in your birth chart, together with your personal archetypes from the Pillars of destiny, and you Flying star.

Furthermore you can identify, your life mission, analyze your Strengths, Weaknesses, Opportunities and Threats, based on the mathematics of I Ching and "Mei Hua Sin I" formula, your best directions and surrounding elements, based on your personal

Gua number, choose your most convenient human compatibility network, and select your best attitude in each moment regarding your flying stars life cycle.

All this information and techniques, will help you to understand your structural and inner issues, together with your relations and social networks.

This understanding is essential to integrate in your life master plan because it will allow you to align and center yourself with your life and inner wisdom, and to manage your life balance in every sector, based on the evaluation made from the magic square "Wheel of Life".

CHECK LIST for PERSONAL FENG SHUI

I - Your Life Hexagram from I Ching and "Mei Hua Sin I"

Number
Line
Main recommendations and SWOT analysis

II - Four Pillars of destiny:

	BRANCH	-	STEM
	YinYang / element		YinYang / element

YEAR Pillar:
MONTH Pillar:
DAY Pillar:
HOUR Pillar:

PILLARS EVALUATION:
- **YIN YANG Balance**

- 5 Elements balance
- Main Harmonious combinations
- Main Clashes

Possible Solutions:

_____

III - Flying Stars & Life cycles

Your Personal Flying Star Number and energy
Basic Archetype
Element
Yin Yang balance

IV - Your Years life cycle

Your Era Number: 8
Your Mansion for the present year:
Your Mansion for the present month:
Main recommendation for attitude:
Next year prospects (Year, mansion and attitude):
Next month prospects (month, mansion and attitude):

V - Others specific consultations:

I Ching
Other Insights

VI – Harmonious relationships:

Golden triangle of Earthly Branches (animal compatibility)
Secret friends
Five elements reinforcing and supportive

J.J. Lupi

CONCLUSION

At personal level you may now calculate and summarized your Heaven's luck, based on the highlights and awareness raised from your destiny evaluation, through the techniques and formulas above.

This reflection aims at understanding yourself, your relations and life cycles, and can be done following the steps and answering the questions below,

> **Locate yourself in your Time Line, to understand your process and evolution,**
> **Identify your main personality, from your Identity to behaviors and context,**
> **Define your targets and well-formed outcomes,**
> **Create an Action Plan with the goals and actions at the levels below,**

You may use the questions and suggestions below for each of the logical levels of operation:

IDENTITY and spiritual path,
    Understand and make sense of it.

VALUES
    Elicit your life VALUES, what's excessive or non-relevant or missing
    ? What is more important in life for you?
    Write it down,
    Prioritize them
    Check what is missing
    Reinforce or introduce it (the help of a professional is recommended)

❖ 256 ❖

BELIEFS, limiting and enhancing BELIEFS
> Check the main five believes that limited your life changes
> ? What objective data confirm this? Check their consistency, and act.
> Check the main five believes that helped you in your life

SKILLS
> I know I cannot do it... but if I could ... what skills would I need? Check those you had before and those you need to access now for the first time

BEHAVIOURS
> Act as if already got what you would like to achieve.

CONTEXT
> Evaluate and adopt your Physical and Human context

Now we recommend you to go back to your Life Plan from Part II, and adapt it based on the highlights above, from your personal Feng Shui map.

PART IV

NEURO FENG SHUI

Life Coaching

ANNEXE: NEURO FENG SHUI, Case Study

Outcome

Further training and information on Neuro Feng Shui

Neuro Feng Shui Coaching

The Technique of Coaching and the Art of Feng Shui
"Art begins where Science ends"

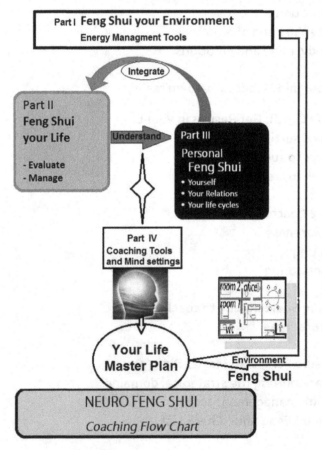

Fig 43

Neuro Feng Shui Coaching

Life Coach for Abundance

*"Intelligence is based on how efficient a species became
at doing the things they need to survive"*
Charles Darwin

Life Coach, is the process of helping you to create a good and
healthy life, not only free of diseases and pain, but full of wellness
and energy, coherent with your mission and vision of life in your
home, work and social environments.

This is the essence of the work of a *Personal Life Coach*, and the
individual you coach is called the *Coachee*. When this individual is
yourself, the process is called *Self Life Coach*.

The essence of coaching is to provide support and tools for change
in a chosen direction. The coach creates awareness, helps to
broaden the choices, fosters change, and does not need to be an
expert in the person's field, because its main function is to provide
the emotional distance for reflection and action over the "changing
process" and allow you be as effective as possible to achieve and
monitor your personal goals.

The key concept, *"if what you are doing does not work, do something
else"* remembers you that you cannot expect something different
if you continue to act as you have always done.

J.J. Lupi

The Life Coach is a personal trainer specialized in the coaching process. He will help his client (coachee), guiding him in to analyze, review, get conclusions, define its goals, decide an action plan, and mostly to act and proceed in the chosen direction in order to achieve his global and specific targets and wishes.

In a simple coaching protocol, you will find in the next chapters how to wrap up the previous information on how to approach your life, access your personal destiny, manage the subtle forces, and to organize a master plan in order to,

- understand
- accept
- change

and then develop a specific path with well-formed outcomes, a valid time frame and monitoring lighthouses.

Finally you will design the Feng Shui solutions for your environment, bringing harmonious surroundings to support your life goals and balance your energy, within your home, work and social network, attracting abundance and fulfillment to your life.

1

Coaching, emotions and stress response

Success people either have a mindset of excellence or they have been programmed as such with techniques available in the area of Neuro Linguistic Programming. Coaching is common in all the sports entertainment, business, and any field of excellence, which demands a perfect coherence between psychology and physiology.

Since the last decades of past century, corporate coaches, team and personal Coaches allow extraordinary performances to individuals, their clubs, teams, groups, companies and even country governments.

Most of these coaches as in football or finances come from old success people in the same field they coach, because they need to know the area so they can develop specific and action programs. These is the most know concept of coach, and is based on getting skills, and capacities.

Coaching in its different modalities, such as Coaching for excellence, Team Coaching, Sports Coaching, Leadership Coaching, Executive Coaching, Personal Trainer (PT) of Health and well- being which are among the most well-known techniques, have developed strategies, tactics and very powerful styles, for each area, but because they often address specific human skills, they often lose track of the whole human being, and its integral life.

Together with the Coaching activity, some other professions emerged, like Mentors, Counselors and even the Holistic Therapy professionals, where the distinctions are not so clear between them. All they pretend to lead people, groups and organizations to their best performance, based on an action plan supported by the power of personal or social commitment, and monitoring.

While therapists focus on changing the basic personal patterns, and mentors and counselors guide you through the change, coaching is focused on results, and this is the main difference between these various professionals. As stated in the "law of attraction", every person's situation is build up through their own set of values, believes, capacities, behaviors and contexts, so most of these professionals focus on the changing process.

Coaching stands for Getting Results, and "Life Coach" stands for "getting results for a life of excellence"!

Most of these techniques are based on the so called behavioral medicine or in Neuro Linguistic Programming (NLP), the "Language of the Mind"!.

The psycho-bio-energetic human being is part of a family and society which he affects and is affected by, in a permanent feedback loop of a full quantum journey, which binds everyone to its whole network of people, things, situations and generations, beyond time and space

The main focus will be to adapt our life style to better react to Stress factors, which are responsible for more than 85% of the chronic "diseases", the loss of well-being and quality of life, together with most of the so called modern health or civilizational problems.

Stress is the biological adaptive response to changes in the environment, which is managed by our (ANS) Autonomic Nervous System. It is perceived as a threat and it manifests as dysfunctions with specific psycho physiological signs and symptoms, very different from a "nervous tension".

Most of our priorities in life are focused in three main areas: my home, my work and social life. All this areas have people, things and situations that influence and frame the conditions where and how we live.

The useful attitude in all situations demand us some of the warrior qualities of courage, patience and intelligence. Courage to change everything we can change to fit our purpose, the patience to accept everything we cannot change, and the intelligence to identify clearly and separate one set from another.

This is how you avoid wasting energy with things that you do not have any influence on, and allow to assemble all your strengths to focus for action over what is within your sphere of influence, so you can be effective, not accepting to live below standards you can change.

E-Motion, stands for setting "in-motion", remembering that the fuel of all your actions, are your emotions. They are the connection between your intellect, what you think, and what you do, or act. Psychic and physically you can see this through the 3 body centers:

- ➢ your heart (emotions),
- ➢ your head (thinking),
- ➢ your body members (moving).

These emotions are generated by an internal process, dependent on your internal representation, or how you perceive things. This is independent from the actual external event or reality. The process to create an emotion is a flow going from your (IR) internal representation, to your (ID) internal dialogue that creates a specific (Ph) physiology, this one closely associated with the emotions they create.

So you can act over your emotions, changing your (Ph) physiology, your (ID) internal dialogue and your (IR) internal representation, of each issue.

The YIN YANG of Emotions

Emotions are your lighthouse on the sea of life. Every emotions as a balance level to be reached, because if you have overdoses or lack of any emotion, it means that there is an issue or message that something is going the wrong way and needs to be harmonized.

We provide you below a list of emotions, that you can classify as Yin or Yang in their essence, and provide solutions if they are in excess or default. Understanding the psychosomatic connections of emotions can be done through the mini guide on mansion 5 of Part II.

To illustrate how you can identify and balance every emotion based on its main root energy, using the concepts of Yin Yang, we analyze below a case of anger and depression.

Anger = Yang emotion

Too much anger needs Yin solutions like calming music to regulate it.

Depression = Yin emotion

Too much depression, needs Yang cures to harmonize it, like sports, bright colors.

Emotions can push your energy up or down ranging from the lowest to the highest vibrational frequency's, they are either YANG or YIN, and can be presented as a scale where you can locate yourself, some pushing you for action, like joy, rage or fear, others making you to withdraw from the public into your inner self, like sadness and guilt.

If you are above the middle the emotional spiral will push you up, if you are in the lower part the emotional spiral will push you down, so we propose you to locate yourself in this scale to understand your actual status.

Body, Mind and Emotions

Our brain has three levels of operation in it basic configuration, the (1) reptilian brain is responsible by our "fight or fly" automatic reaction, and its name comes from our reptiles ancestors and the survival of the faster ones, the (2) limbic system is the emotional brain and also manages the semi-automatic brain responses to any situation.

Finally the (3) Neo-Cortex is the last part developed and manages our rational thinking and our capacity to solve complex issues, this is the part we use to plan, while the other two responses are subconscious or unconscious and should be programmed for perfect operation.

In Feng Shui your Mind, we talk about taken "emotional distance" from the situations to be able to have the right attitude about any issues, without reacting from past experiences and learnings that are mostly out dated.

Through the Psycho Somatic connections we may understand and identify daily situations of people and relate to their states and wellness levels, through the connections between thoughts, emotions, hormones and expressions, as we may see below.

Nr. Thoughts and emotions from Lighter to Heavier energy levels
A. Glands and detoxification organs
B. Words and expressions

Each group starting from the higher energy levels to the lower ones are presented below. ? Where are you now?

N1. Conscientiousness and enthusiasm
A. Skin, Pineal, Hypothalamus
B. I am, I love, I know, I enjoy, I have, I choose, I create

N2. Forgiveness
A-Kidneys and Bladder
B- That was unacceptable, It hurt me long time ago, I will never forget that

N3.Letting go
A-Colon, Large intestine
B-I am out of control, I cannot let go

N4.Pain
A-Pituitary
B-It hurts too much, why did you did this to me?

N5.Anger
A-Thyroid and Parathyroid, Liver and Gall Bladder
B-I hate that, I will get even, I won't, you cannot make me that

N6.Fear
A-Adrenals, Thymus
B-I always worry about things, I need to have it, What if it is wrong?

N7.Grief
A-Pancreas
B-Nobody understands, I feel sad, there is nothing I can do

N8. Apathy
A-Spleen, Lymphatic system
B-I don't feel like it, how will I survive?

N9. Survival
A-Respiratory system
B-How will I survive? I can't get it

N10. Unconsciousness
A-Genitals
B-I am not aware of it, I don't understand

2

Your mind create your reality

The iceberg of our reality, as is show in the figure below illustrate the relationship between our conscious and unconscious mind as a ruler of our drives and main behavior characteristics

In this known diagram of our Conscious/ Unconscious relationship, we can view the minimal impact of your level of consciousness in your daily life, given the depth an unconscious that holds all knowledge of our past, present and future.

Our brain limited capacity to process information is estimated at only 240 bits, from the 2,000,000 bits of information we receive every second. If the latest represents the total objective data, our brain filters through its reticular formation, and retains only a small part of it around 10.000 times smaller. These filters depend on our individual life experience, so creating our unique personality.

Your personality corresponds to your personal identity, and is shaped by values, beliefs, capacities, behaviors, learned from your experiences, and creating the unconscious patterns feeding the part of the brain named "reticular formation", responsible by focusing and retaining some aspects of the information and not others.

Our 3 brains system and personal Time Line

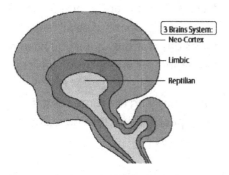

Diagram Conscious versus Unconscious relationship

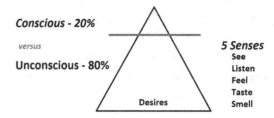

Conscious - 20%

versus

Unconscious - 80%

Desires

5 Senses
See
Listen
Feel
Taste
Smell

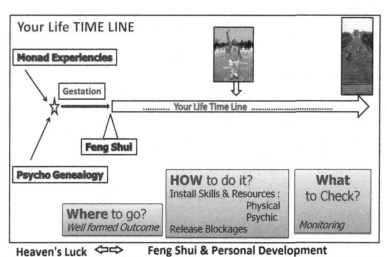

Fig44

Contexts and situations, also condition your reality, for example if you are looking for your blue coat, you will notice every coat and blue things, but will not count any orange stuff, or as when travelling and hungry, you will probably, see all restaurants on the side of the road, and miss gas stations, but if you have no fuel, you will probably miss the restaurants and focus on gas stations.

Therefore every person, even living the same objective experience, will focus on different aspects, thus creating a unique individual reality for one common event.

That is why we cannot expect that the perception of others, "their Map", will be the same as my perception, "my Map", for the same objective experience, which is our "common Territory".

Understanding these inevitable differences and take them in consideration in all your relations and communication processes is the essence of all our happiness, delusions, and Personal Power!

3

Life Coach: Get results in your life

Life Coach with **Neuro Feng Shui**, provides you with the tools to manage your whole life with in an *Integral Coaching Process*, from your Environment and your Identity to all your Life dimensions, within a structure allowing you to *do it as a standalone process.*

You will deal with your rational mind together with your intuition, to understand your time, space and environment and raise your awareness, allowing you the best attitude and planning capabilities. You will also program your unconscious mind responsible for your automatic reactions of your basic limbic and reptilian brain, for the best adaptive response.

As in corporate environment strategy plans, there are also three levels to be taking into account when you define a global action plan for life change, as we will see in the next seven points,

 A. The **S**trategically level, focus in a global view on the Strengths, Weaknesses, Opportunities and Threats (SWOT), presented in your scenario. This level deals mostly with points 1, 2 and 3 below, the "WHERE am I" part,

 B. The "HOW to do it", is the **T**actical level allowing to define the path and the ways that could lead you to your objectives, concerning points 4 and 5 that follows,

C. The Operational part is the "HOW" to get there", and comprises parts 6 and 7, the detailed actions, resources and tools that you will use, to follow the tactical path decided.

Mind setting for success:

The Feng Shui approach to change, is when you start your transformation process, by liberating the energy of a space, through identifying your main energy and those surrounding, and how they affect you.

You clean, unblock, organize the "junk", identify what you want to attract to your life and what you want to get away from. Then you use the "cures", to reinforce and create the new energies you want to have in the right places, and at the same time you counteract or eliminate the old energies you want out of your life.

Keys to succeed:

1. *Identify where we are;*
2. *Presuppositions for a better life,*
   Clear whatever limits us (beliefs, patterns, and limiting decisions).
3. *Well-formed outcomes,*
   Define where we want to go;
4. *Build the skills we need and those that we still do not have;*
5. *Create and assume the behaviors that lead us to the goals;*
6. *Plan time, and create success stories on every step to get there;*
7. *Act!*

Let's analyze each one of this steps to understand how put them in action, in order to *attract abundance in your life* .

1-Identify where you are

Start knowing where you are and in what "direction" you want to go to, through defining your vision and mission. Define and setup your LIFE Compass as we show you in part III.

Align your conscious and your unconscious and avoid the "psychological reversal", where you accept undesirable situations because of secondary gains most of them unconscious, or you stick to your "comfort zones" even if they are usefull no more.

You are attracted to "things, people or situations" which you are programmed to attract. Free yourself of your beliefs and repetitive patterns, change the "program" of your mind!

2- Presuppositions for a better life

- *Identify where your "program" is working against you,*
- You don't make mistakes ... but there is always feedback to your actions.
- You cannot, NOT communicate!
- If your negative beliefs and behaviors have been learned, then you can learn something else,
- Grief, mourning and losses; do your mourning and end your divorces, allow yourself to have what you want in life, free yourself from the chains that no longer bring you progress and pleasure,
- If what you're doing does not work ... do something else!
- Useless or harmful beliefs, are those that harmed you because you believed them when they were told to you often as a child, creating fears and limiting decisions that bind you during a lifetime,

- Your problem will only belong to the past when it is no longer a problem and not when you think that it has already been forgotten. Move on with your life, but do not forget!
- Memories, the famous posttraumatic stress (also known as post-traumatic stress disorder or PTSD) that haunts you throughout life and invade your dreams,
- The capacity of changing the way you experience reality is usually more useful then changing the content of our reality,
- There is a positive intention behind every behavior, and a context where every behavior makes sense,
- Every person is different from its behaviors which may be more or less adequate, depending on their context,
- The Map is not the Territory,
- Every individual has all the resources he needs for change
- Every distinction humans can make about their environment, can be represented through the five senses: vision, hearing, kinestetc, smell and taste,
- Control the time and space: put your Problems in the Past, Live the Present, Plan the Future.

3- Well-formed Goals and Targets

Coaching is about getting results, Life Coaching is about getting results in your life, that is why to define your Goals and Objectives is so important, and you need to do it within some critical conditions for effectiveness, in order to achieve operational **Well Formed Outcomes**.

To do so, your targets need to respect some rules, which allow them to be achieved within the least resistance/maximum efficiency.

These rules state that each objective should be:

Stated positively
Remember that your unconscious do not process negatives.
For example try "don't think about a yellow car"!!! What did you thought at first???

Depending only on yourself
If your goals depend on someone else, how much of it is depending on you?

Evidence of achievement
How do you know when you get it?
What is the last thing that has to happen so you know you got it?

Ecologically with your mind
When will you reach your target,
What do you get that you still don't have?
What will you lose that you have now?
Do you still want it?

What is the first thing you need to do to get it?

What is your Plan B?

After knowing how to define Well-formed Outcomes for your targets, you can proceed to design your action plan.

4- Build the skills we need and those that we still do not have;

Remember all what you have already achieve!

Those skills are still yours, you just need to get in touch with them, through a Psychology and a Physiology of excellence.

List all the skills you never had and you may need to get what you want, and start learning them NOW!

5- Create and assume the behaviors that lead us to the goals;

The Law of Attraction in daily life.

Since you define your goals, you should learn the "rules" of your future surrounding, like behaviors, places, people and their implicit and explicit codes, so you should start since now to be acquainted with them.

Beware of your SSN (Social Support Network): *optimize the life of each person in your life network, and line up your goals with those of your company, your family or your team!*

Synergy: 1 +1 is more than 2

6- Plan time, and create success stories on every step to get there

Define goals compatible with your life scope, and cut every big objective in smaller and easier attainable ones, all well-formed as seen above. This will allow you to go step by step, through the road to success, with every story reinforcing your self-confidence and getting you closer to your final target.

Remember to set up clear monitoring marks so you know when you get there! Most people pass through their objectives without noticing they were already there, except when they leave them again.

7- Act now!

Attitude is everything! In order to optimize your energies, you should avoid the trap of some of the most harmful ones, very present on modern society,

1. Let the past be the past, it only exists through the way on how it affects you today,

2. Create your future instead of depending on it,
3. Live now the present moment, where you can do both:
   - change your past, changing the way it affects you
   - create your future with your present actions and attitudes

How to Create Abundance

Cause or Effect? which side are you on?

When you accept to be the main "cause" of your problems, you call to yourself the "Power" to solve them, because you are at their root cause. Therefore, considering myself "guilty", implies that I am the cause of my own problems, so I can take responsibility and act upon them, in other words, I have power over them!

On the other hand, whenever I position myself on the Effect side "I suffer the effects of external events that I can't control", I withdraw my own power away, so I submit myself to whatever I can't control.

Could it be that you still have that "martyr" attitude of someone to whom everything happens because "others" are to blame, and you are just suffering the EFFECT of their actions?

I am the CAUSE of my life ... and therefore, I can change it. You may now understand that the ability to create the life you want is, exclusively, in your hands!

4

The Coaching Process

In its essence a Coaching process is based on Awareness, Action and Monitoring.

Awareness to bring to conscience the subtle influences and unconscious patterns that run your life and create the reality you are living, so you may learn to become more flexible.

The new highlights on the way you see reality can ease your adaptation process, and provide you other perspectives to move forward.

Unconscious and subtle processes are based, in one hand, in your environment represented by the **Feng Shui**, in another hand, by your **Mind** programs that have been imprinted all along your lifetime, and even before you were born through your psycho-genealogy and family patterns.

They run your life as invisible conditioning forces driving your decisions, reactions and attitudes, through your basic values, beliefs and mind strategies.

These neurological processes are the basis of Neuro Feng Shui coaching. Only Awareness and Acceptance of these factors allow you to take action on them in order to change their impact in your life.

Action can be taken when you have clear *Targets*, the proper *Skills*, together with the needed *Energy or Motivation*. It will be effective when you are committed and compromised with a clear plan to follow.

The *Targets* need to be well formed so you can focus on them and shorten the distance to your goals. Just remember that one off the main issues of your objective is how much you can influence the accomplishment of it. Do not rely on others hands because their priorities are not yours.

The key *Skills* just need to be first identified, and then you may get them from training or practice.

You can find the *energy or motivation* you need, from clear well-formed objectives and through identifying and releasing your secondary gains and comfort zones that suits you no more, to finally get a clear perspective on the end of the road you are heading for, with all its implications.

Monitor your process, is to define evidence based achievements, that tells you how close or far from the road ahead you are.

Finally, the critical question about choosing an expert "Coach" is related to the fact that "nobody can lead you to a place where he has not yet arrived!"

So you need to choose carefully and know where and what you want to achieve, to be able to select the most suitable professional, otherwise you may use this model of Protocol and be your own Self Coach.

That is why we bring this book to you, a guide through your transformation path, so you can take in charge your personal process in a simple but complete and effective way, raising conscientiousness, implementing action and monitoring evolution.

Why Feng Shui in a Coaching process? Actually, the traditional tools of coaches, are mostly based on NLP techniques dealing with rational hard facts, and creating a conscious path to achieve it, through a basic process which is,

> Know where you are
> Know where you want to go
> Decide How to get there

The typical coach will help you to define these three steps and will walk you during the third one, the HOW part of it, which is in essence a conscious process. Meanwhile Feng Shui complements this approach dealing mostly with the subtle and unconscious forces.

Coaches work focused in your mind and tangible forces, forgetting often the subtle energies influencing each process, while Feng Shui experts usually focus more on the subtle and heavenly energy, with independence of the personal conscious mind and environment inner world of each individual.

Feng Shui Your Mind bridges this Gap!

Start by asking the following questions,

? What are you actually doing that you would like to do otherwise? List the main items.
? What would you like to do instead?
? What stops you from doing it?
List the reasons for each item
? Have you done this before?
? What do you need to do it?

From the analysis of the previous answers, you may find what are the priority areas to be dealt with, from your environment in part.I, your life in part.II, your faith and relations in part.III,so you may choose where to start.

The first part of the book provides you the concepts and the tools to analyze space and Feng Shui of the environment, with the resources to sense the subtle forces involved. The in depth look on the life mansions of Lo Shu as a Life Matrix together with the tools to analyze and optimize each of your life domains, is the object of part II.

Personal Feng Shui, is presented in part III, providing you the tools to make a strategically evaluation of your strengths and weaknesses, how you relate with others, how to easily get in touch with your higher self-objectives, assessing and evaluating personalities an human compatibilities, in order to raise your awareness on the different perspectives of each situation.

Furthermore you will be able to access your unconscious knowledge to align yourself with opportunities and threats, recognize the life cycles and phases where you can put your efforts and when to withdraw and recover for the next step.

All these tools will be precious helpers, allowing you to access your full personal power, as soon as you start programming your conscious and unconscious mind to help you with full awareness, instead of holding into the "Veil" of illusion.

The Feng Shui approach of Life, is very consistent with most of modern views and considers the continuum of psycho-genealogy on the family line, and monad experiences before birth, through the gestation process, until the birth moment and following up along the development of your life time, until today and further on.

5

The Feng Shui Upgrade to Coaching

"Life is what happens when you are busy making other plans"

Managing Time and Space allow a huge jump in effectiveness, integrating analyses of the environmental factors and their evolution, and so allowing you to forecast changes and spot fixed environmental factors.

To integrate all these dimensions, Feng Shui adds to the conventional approach to Life Coaching,

- The Space dimension allowing to influence the environment for the best,
- The Time dimension to take into account the permanent evolution of all things, to decide the best moment to act,
- The Subtle Quantum Forces, undetected by formal approaches of conventional coaching,
- The understanding and integration of predestination in life.
- A full Life Matrix, based on the Lo Shu, which has been proved through time,

Procedures

To use Neuro Feng Shui as a Life enhancing tool, you should move step by step, every time analyzing and noting the effect of the changes you made in order to feel comfortable and reassured, creating a record of successes, and adjusting the effects of each action.

In first chapters we introduce you to the tools to evaluate and act over the energies of your environment, your life and your mind, that you will use during the whole process.

Depending on the answers on the end of last chapter 4, you may start by quick checking your environment at home, work and relations, or start from the global issues in part II, and then move inside.

First you can check every aspect of your life with exercises and solutions for analysis and intervention in part II, by fully review and reset your life, step by step and mansion by mansion, each one referring to a domain of life, in which your mind as a definitive influence.

Here we enter the inner space, where you evaluate your health and wellness reviewing the life mansions of the Lo Shu Matrix, and its summarized in the end of part II. Analyze every area or mansion of your "Wheel of Life" based on the same Ba Gua Matrix, use the "cures" and the techniques, proposed in each mansion. Reinforce the effect of each solution using together the physical, the mind and the spiritual levels.

Use the techniques explained before to review your life and reprogram your mind into:

Liberate blockages, limiting believes and decisions on every area
Define your partial objectives, specific to each mansion with welcomed conditions
Broaden your options, the more option the more freedom
Obtain the capacities you may lack to achieve your goals
Set your time frame

Adopt the behaviors and attitude "as if" you already had the goals
Surround yourself of the people and places you will be with when you get it

Resume the Lo Shu matrix and make the general action plan, then detail it by life mansion.

In order to understand better your inner potential and your path in this life, we give you in Part III, the tools to evaluate and understand better who you are, where you come from, your mission and major challenges, your social network, using the time and space approach of Feng Shui.

Now you can use the Personal Feng Shui mathematics, to integrate the time dimension and your life challenges, prepare yourself and choose the most convenient attitude at every moment to your higher good and everything around you.

Next, go back and integrate these findings back in your Life Mansions analysis, and after calculate your life markers from Heaven's luck, review your main life targets, to make them consistent with your personal energy, redesign the action plan for your Life to integrate your personal characteristics and be consistent with your global wellness and life purpose.

Go back to part II and reassess all targets and cures in the light of the personal trends you have found out in the Personal Feng Shui analisys, which is the predetermined part of your life.

Finally go back to Part I, for the next and final step, checking and organizing your environment location and its surrounding areas, then move inside the buildings, your home, work, social and private activities.

Check the main energy through the entrance door, then every room and its purpose regarding to their position on the PA Kua Matrix.

Adjust the Yin Yang, The Elements, activate the cures.

Always remember your intention!

6

Neuro Feng Shui Master Plan

Harmonizing The Strategical Domains

The first tool we use is the reference to the three major domains of influence represent the strategically levels of harmony, influencing your faith:

Heaven
This represents time and the predetermination in life
Human
This area is within your free will and relates to your personal development
Earth
This area also within your free relates to your subtle physical and environmental forces

Using at its best life circumstances for your advantage, demands careful analyses of each one of these domains in order to get the best out of each one.When you calibrate and resonate your life actions and your mind with each of this dimensions, this will allow you to attract success and good fortune.

You will benefit greatly if you consider the earth luck from Feng Shui your environment, to optimize your chances for success, along with your actions and the heaven's luck you usually count on.

Heaven's influence is permanent, since the weather, the atmosphere and air quality, pollution, but also by your birth moment in time and space, your location and birth date, including all the family line psycho-genealogy and soul path, influencing your destiny.

Every synchronic unexpected events in your life, sudden inspirations, lucky chances, fortunate and unfortunate sudden issues, all alignedin a perfect timing, also belong to heaven's domain.

You can find and calculate, most of your heaven destiny in Part III of Personal Feng Shui, and its final summary.

The Human dimension, refers to your all your life situations, as seen in the Feng Shui Matrix of Life in Part II of this book. Here you can find diagnostic methods and intervention tools allowing you to improve your personal development, and positive behavior.

How to analyze and balance your human network which is the people that surround you, and may help you to achieve your projects, your family, relations and associates, and the harmony existing among all, is the subject reviewed in Part III on "Personal Feng Shui", namely across the personal compatibility chapters.

Finally the Earthly dimension or the Feng Shui, refers to everything that supports your environment, and the external and internal energy surrounding you, like food, water, house, location in mountains or seaside, town or country, and is the one most usually forgotten because people are not enough aware of its existing subtle influences.

A detailed reference chart for your surroundings is presented in in Part I on Feng Shui your Environment, and the final chapter gives you a ready to use flow chart to assess and act upon it.

To summarize, the Heaven's timing, the Earth location and the Human life, are the three strategic dimensions you should take into account, and are analyzed in depth in previous chapters. First chapters for Feng Shui of the environment, then in the Part II we analyzed the Human's Life dimensions, and finally the Heaven's luck in part III with personal Feng Shui.

Let's now resume those evaluations, to define and materialize an Action Plan for your life development.

Any action plan should start with an evaluation of the present situation so we will go back to Part II Feng Shui your life, to recover the global Life Matrix evaluation and the detailed analysis for each Life mansion. This will be highlighted by Heaven's luck and Personal energy, and supported by the Feng Shui your Environment Solutions, in order to achieve a full life and personal balance to create Health, Wellness and a Long Life.

7

A Life Management Tool

Neuro Feng Shui Coaching, provides you with a **Life Management Tool** on how to wrap up these resources on an easy protocol to update your life, within the scope of your dreams, and objectives.

This approach needs a mind setting with a clear vision of life and its process, in order to understand how we can apply our efforts for change in the smooth way, with the most effective and maximum impact.

There are four main parts for this protocol that you should follow step by step.

1- Check your life
Your actual life is the result of your past and is preparing your future.

Start from your life's actual evaluation and goals setting as proposed in Part II of this book, through the wheel of life. This area is under your control and depends fully on your free will.

Looking to your Life Feng Shui as proposed in Part II, will define your present situation and objectives, either globally, from the Lo Shu Matrix, or specific to each life Mansion as you check them through the highlights and techniques proposed for each one.

This will allow you to review your main values, beliefs, behaviors and contexts, in order to decide whether or not these have brought you a happy and successful life, and define new targets and corrective actions.

Here is where Personal Development is the key to succeed.

2- Personal Feng Shui, the heavenly luck.
Understand your destiny settings, life cycles, and your relations affinities.

Next, we give access in Part III, to the mathematics of your life prospects, with a full SWOT (Strengths, Weaknesses, Opportunities and Threats) analysis, that will help you to understand where you came from, where you are and where you go, through the calculations of your life path, key issues and archetypes.

This Heavenly information allow you to check whether you are consistently connected and centered with your life mission and spiritual path, together with and introduction to the time cycles where you can prepare to wait or act, optimizing the best chances for success..

The challenge here is how to accept and integrate these different aspects that will allow you to live a coherent and fulfilled happy life. This is the predetermined part of your life that you should better accept is out of your control, and integrate it harmoniously, in your unconscious mind.

A perfect time management, understanding impermanence, life cycles and the energy of each period will let you choose wisely whether to act or hold back in the right moment to avoid stress and wasting energy, so to have the most "useful attitude" in every moment of your life.

Last but not least, you will learn to spot your relations affinities, allowing you to choose a human supportive and harmonic network.

3- Review your life and setup your Goals
Life and personal settings

The previous evaluations will provide you some information allowing to better understand and accept your life challenges, and how they fit into a learning process for evolution, so you may review and adjust the conclusions of your Life Feng Shui defined initially

Now we recommend you to go back to your Life Plan, in number 1 above, and adapt it based on the highlights of your personal Feng Shui map, and findings.

4- Your environment and earthly issues
Space management, through the external and internal Feng Shui.

Finally, Feng Shui is the last frontier where you can create the environmental supporting energies for the goals you set in the previous approaches, also it is one area, depending on mostly on your free will to adjust your life. Remember that your human environment is a major part of it also.

Set up the environment to help, with people, things and situations surrounding you.

Neuro Feng Shui
4 steps Operational
Check List

PERSONAL DATA:

Name
Birth Date
Birth Time
Birth Place

YOUR ENVIRONMENT

WHERE DO I LIVE?

Adress:

Do I please myself with the weather, the atmospheric conditions, pollutions, safety and location?

THE HUMAN NETWORK

How is my harmony (from 0 to 10) with the people surrounding me at:

Work
Business partners
Home
Intimate Relations
Social relations

1. Check your Life

Belonging to the Human realm, we will use the information from part II to evaluate your Wheel of Life and assess your main difficult areas to balance Life Mansions and define first targets,

- *Identify the main mansions or areas where you are not comfortable*
- *Clarify the issues from each of the problematic mansions*
- *Propose general possible corrective actions*

Where are you now ?

From the resume of Part II, where you have checked your life through the path of your Life mansions, pick up the general evaluation in the end of it and place it here below. We will use the Lo Shu Matrix of your wheel of life to get a proper and complete perspective of the actual moment.

First mark the level of satisfaction over the wheel, ranging from 0- totally unsatisfying to 10-totally satisfying

Checking your Life Mansions

4	9	2
Power & Abundance	Fame & Image	Partners Relationships
3	**5**	**7**
Origins NuclearFamily Psycho-genealogy	Health Main Energy	Criativity Children
8	**1**	**6**
Knowledge Spirituality	Career & Life Projects	Mentors Helpers

Mansion - Value

Mansion	Value
3	-
4	-
5	-
6	-
7	-
8	-
9	-
1	-
2	-

Fig 45

Now
1) resume for each area in three words,
2) the actual situation and
3) the next target you want to reach in that area.

Use all your unlimited creativity for the wording....

MANSION 3, number of satisfaction level (0 to 10):
1
2
3
MANSION 4, number of satisfaction level (0 to 10):
1
2
3
MANSION 5, number of satisfaction level (0 to 10):
1
2
3
MANSION 6, number of satisfaction level (0 to 10):
1
2
3
MANSION 7, number of satisfaction level (0 to 10):
1
2
3
MANSION 8, number of satisfaction level (0 to 10):
1
2
3
MANSION 9, number of satisfaction level (0 to 10):
1
2
3

MANSION 1, number of satisfaction level (0 to 10):

1

2

3

MANSION 2, number of satisfaction level (0 to 10):

1

2

3

2. Personal Feng Shui, the heavenly luck

Time and destiny belong to Heaven's luck and from the tools we gave you in Part III you can access this information, allowing you to have a clear perspective on your life events, your destiny and make sense of your past difficulties as part of the learning process to accept the lessons and keep the track on you path.

At personal level, you will need to calculate based on the formulas of Part III, the following values to highlight and understand your personal life path.

2.1- Your Life Directions

Calculate your 4 Best,

.

.

.

.

and Worst directions,

.

.

.

.

2.2- Your Life Hexagram from I Ching and "Mei Hua Sin I"

Number
Changing Line
Main recommendations and SWOT analysis

2.3- Four Pillars of destiny

YEAR Pillar:
MONTH Pillar:
HOUR Pillar:
YIN YANG Balance
5 Elements balance
Main Solutions

2.4- Flying Stars & Life cycles

Your Personal Flying Star Number and energy
Basic Archetype
Element
Yin Yang balance

2.5- Your Years life cycle

Your Era Number: 8 for the current Era until 2024
Your Year Mansion:
Your Month Mansion:
Main recommendation for attitude:
Next year prospects (year mansion and attitude)

2.6- Others specific consultations:

I Ching
Other Insights

2.7- Human relations

Golden triangle
Secret friends
Supportive 5 elements

3. Review your Life and set up myour goals

Now we recommend you to go back to your Life Plan and adapt it based on the new conscience, acceptance and integration of the highlights of your personal Feng Shui map, together with the information below.

3.1- Define your Life Compass: *A first step to clarify your Specific Goals*

A life compass are two simple Sheets of Paper where you write, in each one with different colors, your actual perception of your life directions.

Set up your "LIFE Compass"

Pick up 2 white sheets of paper, one pen red and one blue and make the exercise from page 129 on part II Mansion1.

- Keep the two sheets in your wallet and check it and adapt it once in a while, with a minimum once a week.

Select and Write down now, the 5 life issues that:

you want to go towards

_____

you want to move away from

_____

3.2- WELFORMED Outcomes

In these integration phase, you should define what personal development strategies you need, and how to use the techniques proposed in each mansion to cope with adaptations you may need at the different levels from Identity to behavior and context.

Some preliminary evaluations should consider,

> **Elicit your life VALUES and what's missing, excessive or non-relevant,**
> ? What is more important in life for you?
> Write it down,
> Prioritize them
> Check what is missing
> Reinforce or introduce it (the help of a professional is recommended)
>
> **Limiting and enhancing BELIEFS**
> Check the main five believes that limited your life changes
> ? What objective data confirm this?
> Check the main five believes that helped you in your life
>
> **SKILLS**
> I know I cannot do it... but if I could ... what would skills I need?
> Check those you had before and those you need to access now for the first time

BEHAVIOURS
Act as if already got it.

CONTEXT
Evaluate and change your Physical and Human context

General Life Goals, timing and markers of success

Goals for each relevant Mansion, timing and markers of success

- **Mansion 3**

- **Mansion 4**

- **Mansion 5**

- **Mansion 6**

- **Mansion 7**

- **Mansion 8**

- **Mansion 9**

- **Mansion 1**

- **Mansion 2**

The Monitoring process, is of outmost importance, because it allow to set up the milestones where you can check your progresses and pave your "road to success".

MANSION Nr.		Global value =		
	Value 0 to 10	Welformed Outcome Name	Time to Goal	End Value
3				
4				
5				
6				
7				
8				
9				
Totals:				

Define a feasible time schedule for each target that allows you to create a "Path of Success Stories", that will illustrate the achievements and progress you have made.

Within your time schedule, define:

What markers for monitoring the process
Quantify the markers
Define the time range of each target

4. Feng Shui your environment and Earthly issues

Based on your life analyses and action plan, you can now evaluate your environment Feng Shui and define what energies you will need to support your goals. After investigating the physical environment energies, you can then promote the "cures" and solutions that supports you better.

Remember the ancient secret for the effectiveness of the cures and solutions you adopt, you will need to manifest it through the three main levels:

Intention
Speak
Action

4.1- THE HUMAN NETWORK

Best earthly branches
Best supportive elements
Yin / Yang balance

4.2- ENVIRONMENTAL SOLUTIONS

<u>The External Environment</u>
Previous history of the location
Geopathology
Entrance door

<u>Internal Environment</u>
Ba Gua Location of main house areas Strengths and Weaknesses
Kitchen
Bed room
Living room
Toilets
Office

<u>General FENG SHUI Solutions</u>
Energy quality and quantity
5 Elements cures
Yin Yang cures
Ba Gua cures for specific rooms and mansions

<u>Other energetic cures</u>
Lights
Mirrors
Plants
Symbols
Others

Main room of the house, and specific Cures and solutions to implement:

Solution 1:

    Type of solution and tools
    Intention
    Affirmation

Solution 2:

> **Type of solution and tools**
> **Intention**
> **Affirmation**

Solution 3:

> **Type of solution and tools**
> **Intention**
> **Affirmation**

Solution 4:

> **Type of solution and tools**
> **Intention**
> **Affirmation**

Solution 5:

> **Type of solution and tools**
> **Intention**
> **Affirmation**

8

A Final Word - a magical Sentence...

Beware of your words, because they contain a powerful energy! Listen to what you say...

Stop the negative messages that you tell yourself.

Positive affirmations work because they give permission to the subconscious to process the ideas you want.

The power of affirmations

Affirmation statements need to comply with some rules to be effective, and their effectiveness is based on the ability of our unconscious to learn from repetition... " a lie repeated 1.000 times will became true", so you don't need to believe them, just note your reactions when you say them out loud, to allow you to register your weekly evolution. Just repeat them daily, using the following rules,

1. Stated in positive

Remember that the unconscious learns through repetition, and does not process the negative.

"Do not think of a blue elephant!"
- What did you think of?

Think of the results "what you WANT, not what you don't want! Watch it when you say,

· "I do not **want to be fat!"**
· "I do not **want to smoke** anymore!"
· "I'm not **going to eat** any **more chocolates**!"

How about programming your mind with positive affirmations, such as:

· I want to be thinner.
· I want to quit smoking.
· I want to stop eating chocolate.

And if we add to that a clear, quantified and timed goal?

· I want to be thinner, 3 pounds, in 15 days.
· I want to quit smoking and run 3 times a week, starting next week.
· I want to stop eating chocolates and get rid of my zits by next week

!!! How does the image look? Does it look clearer and more appealing?

2. Be specific

Generalities are less effective and subject to brain manipulations, so try to use the principles of well-formed outcomes seen previously, for maximum effectiveness.

3.Refer to the present moment

Your unconscious obeys you exactly as you order. If you put and objective into the future it will stay there forever.

Listen to what you say and you will see the distance to your objective:

"I am thinking about doing it..."
"I decided to do it,..."
"I will do it,..."
"I am doing it,..."

How to use affirmations

List all your priority affirmations and speak them out loud in front a mirror daily.

Take note of your reactions, and evaluate them weekly.

To decide on your best affi rmation, you may use the following process,

1. Accept the problem
2. State it specifically
3. Separate the problematic behavior from yourself
4. Define a phrase where you state the problem and separate it from your self:
"*even though* I am obese, **I totally love and accept myself**"

EXERCISE *OF THE MAGIC SENTENCE*

Do this exercise and use its magic whenever you find yourself in stressful situations!

1.   *Put yourself in a state of Power.*

You can either be naturally under an intense spontaneous and appropriate state or you can induced one, using *the body position, touch and/or the magic word, as you will learn hereafter!*

It is very important to review the situation in the part of your body you felt it, looking at it through your own eyes.

Setup the "Anchor"

Choose a moment where you can be alone with nobody to disturb you. Relax ... you may close your eyes ... make this simple but powerful exercise:

- Remember a time when you were totally happy, thinking that the world was yours.
- As you go back to that time enter in your body and see what you saw with your own eyes, hear what you heard and feel what you felt back then, back when you found yourself in a "power" state.
- A little before the summit of this state of power...for 5 to 15 seconds, press your left wrist and pronounce a statement (a strong and short word or phrase)
- Now get out of this state... Go to the kitchen or sit back on the couch... or ask yourself something that makes you think of something else... (for example: what's your phone number back forward?)

2. *Test of the Sentence - by pressing your wrist in exactly the same way and pronouncing the word / phrase, see if you can go back to the power state.*

3. *If at first it does not work; do it again! Its effect increases with the number of times the "anchor" is triggered.*

Accept that the power to transform your life is only in your mind. Choose NOW, to make each moment of your life a great one and enjoy it!

ANEXE

Case Study
NEURO FENG SHUI

LIFE COACH
IN
5 STEPS

Formulas, calculations and results

LUCY, 42
Born in Paris, November 17, 1972 ate 02:04h AM

Lucy is an intelligent and successful woman, with a career in the public administration and private practice as social helper. She lives in the country capital city, where she pleases herself with the cultural environment has well as the social life and groups of friends, also at the time she was willing to find another home in the same city.

She arrived at her middle age with the dissatisfaction and anxiety appearing usually in moments of major life challenges and change.

This process brought also confusion, which is a prerequisite to loosen the rigid set of values and beliefs, associated with the resistance to change and so allowing the flexibility to find other ways and attitudes more useful for better life.

So applying the Feng Shui your Mind protocol we analyzed 5 steps,

<u>1rst Step – Mapping the general situation</u>

A-Feng Shui check-up
A major hindrance found as there was a WC in the abundance area of the house

B-Using the Part II and the Wheel of Life Matrix
Here she detected that there are some areas evaluated less than 5, for a Global average score of **7**

$(3 \text{ Mansion} \times 10) + (1 \text{ Mansion} \times 9) + (1 \text{ Mansion} \times 6)$
$+ (\textbf{4 Mansion} \times \textbf{4}) = 61$
$61 / 9 = 7 \textbf{ (average value)}$

Meaning that her life is actually 70% satisfactory.

The sensible mansions 3, 4, 5, 8 and 2, have some general issues where the main goals where:

- **Mansion 3: Family relation with her parents**
  Relation with mother with misunderstandings

  <u>General Objectives:</u>
  better understanding and family unity

- **Mansion 4: Money and abundance**
  Need to increase income to allow for more traveling
  Develop further the private practice
  Change from public to private sector in the medium term

  <u>General Objectives:</u>
  Engage in a Master degree at university
  Increase income
  Make one major travel a year

- **Mansion 5: Health**
  Increase flexibility and avoid low back pain

  General Objectives:
  Start two times a week a Yoga class and one Pilates, starting next month
  Psycho somatic causes low back pain: Fear for lack of financial support
  Daily affirmation for 1 month: "life itself supports me, I trust the Universe"

- **Mansion 8**: Knowledge and spirituality
  Develop higher studies
  Get more traveling and time for study and spiritual development

  General Objectives:
  Engage in a Master degree at university
  Get 2 afternoons a week for study and spiritual development

- **Mansion 2: Relations and partnerships**
  No stable intimate relations and lack of business partnerships

  General Objectives:
  Wish for different type from previous ones
  Wish to establish partnerships for her private activity

2d Step – Understanding your personal story and inner drives

Based on Part III of Heaven's destiny, life path, and time management: the Personal Feng Shui.

2.1-   Life Directions

Gua Nr. 5 (feminine 2 West group)
Year 1972, so 7+2= 9 and 9+5= 14
1+4=5, but as Gua 5 is central and as no direction, for a feminine person it belongs to the West group

Best directions, from best of to 4th best:
NE, *Generating breat*
W, *Heavenly doctor*
NW, *Relationships Longevity and Health*
SW, *Development*

Worst directions, from least bad to worse:
E, *Harm*
SE, *Five ghosts*
S, *Six Killings*
N, *Total loss*

Conclusions for action:

According to her previous priorities, she should take special care to enhance and face the following directions,

Generating breat for success, prosperity, vitality, recognition and respect.

Heavenly doctor, for confidence, security, patience and good health

Relationship,s Longevity and Health, for self confidence and reliability, harmony in the family and relationships

Beware of the direction ***Five ghosts, associated with risks of*** prejudice from loss of income, together with quarrels and misunderstanding at home and work. Avoid place cooker in this location.

2.2-   *Your Life Hexagram from I Ching and "Mei Hua Sin I"*

Hexagram of your Life Path:

Upper Trigram: 6
(1972/12) => R= 4
Month: Nov = 11
Day = 17
(4+2+8)= 14 /8 => **R= 6 Water**

Lower Trigram:
Hour: 02:04h => 2
(4+2+8+2)= 16 /8 => **R= 0 or 8 Earth**

Hexagram Number: (6 X 8) from grid Fig 29 => Hexagram 8, The Union

This Hexagram is about a life with a focus on grouping, holding together, union and humility, and talks about nothing negative or definitive, meaning a life discrete and modest but with social focus, which is already the professional path chosen.

Changing line

(4+2+8+2)= 16 /6 => **R= 4**

This line gives a specific advice in professional terms, to stay together with talented people, and if you consider somebody as a mentor, do not hesitate to follow him and ask for advice, but doing so you should not behave diferent after or follow different ways.

Conclusion: main recommendations and SWOT analysis

So far Lucy is well aligned professionally with her mission and path of life, but still needs to find the helpers and mentors she needs to support her.

2.3-   Four Pillars of destiny

YEAR Pillar:
Branch: (1972 / 12) => R= 4, (Zi) RAT,   Yang Water
Stem: (9) Ren,   Yang Water

MONTH Pillar (see Fig 33):
Branch: Nov 17   (Hai) PIG,   Yin Water
Stem: (8) Xin,   Yin Metal

DAY Pillar:
$$\frac{5(X-1) + (X-1)/4 +15 + Y}{60} = D$$
Birth Date: 1972 November 17
X= 72
Y= (31+29*+31+30+31+30+31+31+30+31+17)= 322
*Leap year with February with 29 days

Formula:
$\underline{5(72-1) + (72-1)/4 +15 + 322}$ / 60 = (355 + 17 + 15 + 322) / 60 =
709 / 60 = 11
709 / 60 = 11 with a reminder of 49
D= 11
R = 49

Now lets calculate ;
STEM of the day: 49 / 10 = Reminder 9, so "REN Stem"
BRANCH of the day: 49 / 12 = Reminder 1, so "Zi or RAT Branch"

Resuming the Day Pillar.
Branch: Nov 17   (Zi) RAT,   Yang Water
Stem: (9) REN,   Yang Water

HOUR Pillar:
Branch: 02:40H   (Chou) OX,   Yin Earth
Stem: (8) Xin,   Yin Metal

YIN YANG Balance (4 Yin, 4 Yang)
Good balance although there is a concentration specific to each Pillar, Year pillar is totally Yang, Month pillar totally Yin, Day pillar totally Yang, and hour pillar totally Yin.

5 Elements balance (Water 5, Metal 2, Earth 1, Wood and Fire 0)
No Wood, no Fire, too much water, this could mean too much emotions, and lack of action drive, but this analysis should check specific elements in each pillar and their significance.

2   **Year Pillar**: Family background and society.
Excess Yang and Water
3   **Month Pillar:** Your early childhood and relationship with parents.
Excess Yin and lack of Wood and Fire
4   **Day Pillar:** The (DM) daymaster and relationship with partner/spouse.
Excess yang and Water
5   **Hour Pillar:** Relationship with children, your career and old age.
Excess Yin and lack of Wood and Fire

Main Solutions

Needs to balance the excess water namely in the family and relationships area, with more action and development of projects in life to succeed in career. Also reinforcing Earth element would give more center and stability.

Finaly concerning relations and partnerships, she should consider the good relations with Rat, Dragon and Monkey, all Yang characters reinforcing her missing elements, and Ox her secret friendship reinforcing the earth and consolidation of energy. Tigers, snake, rooster, dog and pig, are options, but beware of horses, rabbit and sheep, for partnerships.

2.4-   Flying Stars & Life cycles

Your Personal Flying Star Number and energy, is Star 1

- **Basic Archetype**

The water star of the north

Flexible like water, sometimes a little too much, they can be deep and active, or turbulent and agitated as a lake or a river or a cascade. Free spirits, they care about their personal space, are sentimental creative, artistic and philosophers. These personalities are quite adaptable and an easy follower, that should cultivate happiness and optimism, paying special attention to their human environment because of its strong influence over their life's. Great mediators, after a usually difficult family childhood, its best period will be around 40's where they should take some resources for older times.

Very sensible to their relations, they have stable relationships, with a passionate and sexual focus.

The body liquids, and their organs, also bones and nerves, should be payed special attention.

- **Elements**

Water again, reinforces an excessive emotional personality, that should learn how to manage these emotional emphasis.

- **Yin Yang balance**

North represents a Yin energy, so reinforcing the balance of the Yang pillars and the unbalance of Yin pillars.

2.5- *Your Years life cycle*

Your Era Number: 8 for the current Era until 2024
Your Year Mansion for 2013: Mansion 1
Main recommendation for attitude:

It is hard to expand in winter time, so no action is favored, but instead a time for preparing, structure and organize. The deep inner secrets personal and illicit may be revealed. Beware of everything related with liquids, water, alcohol, and others.

You may feel isolated, and excluded from others, hidden below the water, so it is the time to explore our inner issues, cultivate the spirit, and meditate on future actions. Control yourself and accumulate strength for the next step.

This is the winter season, where you need to make your analysis, reflections, plans, and beware of unpredictable health and financial problems that may arrive. Only new beginnings of studies are favored together with all sorts of introspections. Elements and stars in conflict related to numbers (earth) 2, 5, 8 and (fire) 9.

Next year prospects and attitude (location in mansion 2):

This is the recollection phase. Now is the moment to materialize what was planned in Mansion 1. Set up and go, letting new plans, creativity, social and economic developments, for the moment and give birth to what was planned. Avoid anxiety and negativity that may arise.

Learn how to accept life routine and enjoy it, without wishing to lead it. Avoid eating to much and take note and manage of your emotional states, without putting yourself in the front line. Elements and stars in conflict related to numbers (water) 1, and (wood) 3,4, are more prone to changes then other stars.

2.6-   *Others specific consultations:*

CHI Numbers in the Magic Square:

Missing numbers 4, 5, 6 creates a weakness arrow of suspicion, which means that there is a suspicious character she should beware of and balance to reinforce the potential for harmonious and stable relations.

3rd STEP – Clarify your goals and find solutions

Going now back to your Life Plan and adapt it based on the new conscience, acceptance and integration of the highlights of your personal Feng Shui map.

Define your Life Compass, is a *A first step to clarify your Specific Goals*

WRITE now the 5 life issues that:
You want to go towards
- Spiritual growth
- Stable healthy relation
- Academic and professional recognition
- More Traveling and leisure time
- Flexibility and healthy spine without pain

You want to move away from
> The routine of public work
> Toxic and codependent relations
> Social isolation
> Professional pressure
> Professional stagnation

WELFORMED Outcomes
Goals for each relevant Mansion, timing and markers of success,

- **Mansion 3: Family relation with her parents**
  Relation with mother with misunderstandings

  Specific Objectives:
- Create a monthly routine to visit the parents and root family, starting from next month.
- Create a new communication approach using the emotional assertive model and checking the preferential channels of each member of the family, accepting the different views of the parents as another approach, without feeling personally attacked or juged

- **Mansion 4: Money and abundance**
  Need to increase income to allow for more traveling
  Develop further the private practice
  Change from public to private sector in the medium term

  Specific Objectives:
- Engage in a Master degree at university this year
- Increase income, through developing my private practice with 4 consultations a week.
- Increase income, through getting a scholarship by the beginning of next year
- Make one major travel a year, starting with a jornay to India next spring.

- **Mansion 5: Health**
- Increase flexibility and avoid low back pain

  Specific Objectives:
- Start two times a week a Yoga class and one Pilates, starting next month

- **Mansion 8: Knowledge and spirituality**
  Develop higher studies
  Get more traveling and time for study and spiritual development

  Specific Objectives:
  - Engage in a Master degree at university next season
  - Reserve two afternoons a week for study and spiritual development

- **Mansion 2: Relations and partnerships**
  - No stable intimate relations and lack of business partnerships

  Specific Objectives:
  Identify where I have previously found the most interesting people in life
  Visit these places two times a week
  Participate every month in one event related to my professional practice from september on

4rth Step – Feng Shui your mind

Revision of the ACTION PLAN FOR YOUR LIFE based on Part IV

Define what personal development strategies you need, and how to use the techniques proposed in each mansion to cope with adaptations you may need at the different levels from Identity to behavior and context.

Elicit your life VALUES and what's missing, excessive or non-relevant,

Conclusion:

> ➤ The value for money was not present in my structure of values
> ➤ The service to others had high priority regarding to value myself

Limiting and enhancing BELIEFS

The parents are always right, because they know better

Marriage is the only form of a stable relationship

NB: Both did not resist to a deep consistency checking, so you may change them for more positive and liberating ones.

SKILLS

Need to do some NLP training on Charisma enhancement and assertive communication

BEHAVIOURS

I will review my dressing code and act as if already got the status I want, and go to the places I would enjoy to go, since now.

CONTEXT

I will change my social and fitness club, and will find some different social groups to add to my social support network.

The Monitoring process, is of outmost importance, because it allow to set up the milestones where you can check your progresses and pave your "road to success".

The Time frame and well-formed outcomes have already been set above for the four relevant life mansions.

<u>5thStep – Manage your environment Feng Shui</u>

Check and reorganize your environment and your social and professional human network: Part I and Part III, environment and personal Feng Shui.

Action Plan, "Check List", for home and workplace

After analyzing the house location and its main areas and matching them with the life's strengths and weaknesses, we designed the follow detailed action plan for the case study of Lucy explained fully hereafter.

The Feng Shui for your Home and Work environment, should focus on solutions to help you to achieve the objectives defined for a full life balance or to achieve some specific goals.

At the same time you will focus on balancing the five elements and the Yan/Yang of your basic nature evaluated in your Personal Feng Shui, that representing your heaven's luck or determinism in your life.

For Lucy's case study, this means mostly reduce the excessive water associated with emotions, and promote wood and fire, related to activity and external image, together with reinforcement of a strong center with element earth, to consolidate and give a solid basis to all possible developments.

Furthermore, you should correct any hindrances associated with the actual location of home and work, with the necessary Feng Shui solutions.

So the following solutions would be recommended after analyzing her home and work location.

Feng Shui the external environment

Environmental and location solutions

Geopathology
The bed should be moved to another position to avoid one Star Point, and one Hartman cross, possibly causing some low back pain she complaints about, also related with material insecurity, associated with the lumbar area of the spine.

Entrance door
Too many furniture in the main entrance hall blocks the entrance preventing people and good energy to enter freely. These need to be removed, to amplify the gateway or the mouth of the Chi.

Closing the access to the main road of the "hidden door" will change the entrance and so the energy of the house from area 6 "helpers and mentors" to the area 8 where is knowledge and spirituality, more in accordance with the new objectives defined.

Internal Environment

Ba Gua Location of main house areas Strengths and Weaknesses

Kitchen
Using the hoven looking towards the entrance or one of your best directions would help income and abundance.

Bed room
- Change the bed to be in the power position or the control zone of the bedroom, instead of the actual position back to the entrance door, allowing things to go on without she notice it

- Avoid the head of the bed to rest against the wall of the WC, and the associated drain of energy during the night

Living room
Reinforcing colors green and red, will counteract the excess of water, and the usage of the peach color and some paired figures, in area 2 will improve and attract relations into your life.

Use green plants and red and yellow flowers, to enhance the wood element that controls water in the 5 elements cycle, and promotes fire. This would be the key element for balancing the elements in the house.

Toilets
Allways keep the door closed and put big mirror on the main external wall of the WC to stop abundance to be draied out

Office
Select the position of your desk according to your best directions and the room control zone, allways keeping an open view over the door, even if you need to use a mirror for that.

OUTCOME

Now that you get the tools, make yourself a priority for you.

Time and Space are the four dimensions of life (3D plus time), so if you don't have time and space for yourself, you do not exist!

Find a place exclusive for yourself at home, take 20 minutes a day, and start to change your life.

Do it Now!

FURTHER TRAINING AND INFORMATION ON NEURO FENG SHUI COACHING

All the subjects of this books have further training for users and professionals through Seminars and On-line courses in Latin America, Europe and Asia.

For further information and subscription please contact:

www.neurofengshui.com
jjlupi@jjlupi.com
www.jjlupi.com
FB: books jj lupi

ABOUT THE AUTHOR

J.J. Lupi
Eng, Master of Sciences, ND

President of the Ibero American Association for Quantum Healing, researcher and coordinator professor in the Faculty of Fortaleza in Brazil, manages the international network of Neuro Quantum Institute, and is the CEO of Quantum Neuro Asia.

Engineer and Master of Sciences from the University of Louvain in Belgium, specialist in human development, with published scientific studies across Europe, mostly on advanced technologies for health and education, coordinates a worldwide network of training and staff development in the use of Neuro Biofeedback, Electrophysiology and Bioresonance in Europe, Latin America and Asia.

Author translated in several languages, namelly with "Communication and Influence with NLP, the secret beyond words", "EFT, the tapping technique of emotional healing at your fingertips", "Neuro Feng Shui, Coaching for the Soul", coordinates the collection "The Power of the Quantum Mind".

Creator of the *Neuro Feng Shui Coaching* process, has a regular practice and contributions to specialized publications that frame the courses and lectures provided in different countries worldwide.

Fluent in five languages, lives between Europe, Brasil, and China.